*Woman's Institute Hall*

Where those who come from out of town to assist the Institute in its mission of helping women everywhere may share in the happiness that results from ideal home surroundings and pleasant companionship.

The image you see above was the illustration from the May 1920, *Inspiration* newsletter that was published by the Woman's Institute of Domestic Arts and Sciences which inspired my book *Vintage Notions*. This was the original building that housed the Institute before they moved to their permanent home, in 1921. For a more modern look, I chose to update this edition with the cover artwork from the Summer 1925 issue of Woman's Institute *Inspiration* magazine.

Edited by GUSTAVE L. WEINSS

# Between Ourselves

## BY THE EDITOR

THIS issue of INSPIRATION comes to you printed on a poorer **grade** of paper than we have been accustomed to using. Possibly most of you are aware that a real serious paper shortage exists in this country. At any rate, the situation is so critical that the publishers of several big magazines are compelled to save paper by combining two issues, by cutting down the number of pages, or by curtailing subscription production.

For a time during the recent railroad strike, we thought that we could not publish the May issue of INSPIRATION. Luckily, however, we were able to procure the paper we are using this time, and we are delighted to think that we do not have to disappoint you entirely. There is an old saying to the effect that "Half a loaf is better than none." In our predicament, INSPIRATION on another grade of paper is better than no INSPIRATION at all.

FOR our cover design, we are showing a picture of Woman's Institute Hall. Ever since the Institute was started, women and girls have been coming to our city from other sections of the country to assist us in carrying on our work. At times it has been a serious problem to find attractive and congenial places where they might live. But recently we were able to take definite steps toward procuring and furnishing a home for them.

Institute Hall, which was formerly the home of a prominent Scranton family, will accommodate thirty-six people with comfort. The interior has been remodeled, redecorated, and entirely refitted to meet the needs of those who will reside there.

As you know, an institution of the magnitude of the Woman's Institute cannot depend entirely on one city for its staff, so as more out-of-town women come to us, we aim to provide other desirable homes for their use, homes in which they may live as reasonably and as contentedly as possible.

HAVE you ever heard of the Government school at Quantico, Virginia? Well, I'll tell you about it. It is called the United States Marine Corps Institute. Here our Government is engaged in teaching thousands of our Marines trades and professions so that when they re-enter civil pursuits they will be equipped with knowledge that will put them on a higher plane and enable them to increase their earnings. We are interested in this great school for two reasons—because it is teaching trades and professions with the aid of the instruction papers prepared and used by the International Correspondence Schools and because it is teaching cookery from the instruction papers prepared and used by the Woman's Institute.

It should be a source of as much gratification to you as it is to us to know that we have lessons that meet the requirements of a school destined to do so much good. And they do meet all requirements, for one of the Generals in charge on a recent visit to the Institute assured us that "they made a rigid and thorough search for textbooks and found no others so admirably suited to their needs as those of the I.C.S. and the Woman's Institute."

SPEAKING about books reminds me of another instance in which a product of the Institute has come to the fore. "The Secrets of Distinctive Dress," with which many of you are familiar, has been adopted as a textbook by the Michigan Agricultural College for its classes in domestic arts. And it is serving its purpose there so well that several other colleges expect to use it.

Of course, we rejoice when a product of our own merits recognition. But that alone is not the reason. What we are most happy about is the fact that the books we offer to our students are backed up not only by what we claim, but by what others—and good authority, too—admit in such a practical way.

ONE more thing I want to talk about is the future home of the Institute. You surely remember the picture we showed you in March INSPIRATION. Well, the foundation of this handsome structure is under way. Everything is hustle and bustle, and, barring unavoidable delays, another month will show the foundation ready for the superstructure.

And then we shall have cornerstone-laying exercises. You know, when a building of this kind is erected, the laying of a cornerstone is strictly in order. This will prove a gala event for the Institute staff, for the winners of the trip to Scranton, as well as for students and friends who live in our vicinity. It is to be regretted that all Institute students cannot participate, but that, of course, would be impossible. In an early issue of INSPIRATION we hope to tell you all about these exercises, so that you will at least feel that, though far apart, we are united by the friendship that comes from working together for the good of all.

# Procrastination *and* Indecision

*By* MARY BROOKS PICKEN
Director of Instruction and Principal of
School of Dressmaking and Tailoring

THE Japanese proverb, "Be not lenient with your own faults; keep your pardon for others," is an exceptionally good one to remember when one is tempted to procrastinate.

A little after 4 o'clock the other afternoon I left my office, and as I went out I heard a girl say, "Oh, it is too late tonight. I'll get after it tomorrow." I walked scarcely a block down the street when I heard a young man say to another, "It's late now, suppose I do that tomorrow." I went directly to the office of a man who is one of the most successful men in our city and as a result one whose time is very precious. I mentioned some things that should be done. His answer was, "We will decide them right now." And as each point was brought up, decisions were made and progress regarding each problem was made possible.

LACK of decision is the subtle germ of procrastination. It is always easy to go ahead after you have decided how you will proceed. For instance, to make a dress, you do not have to be seated at the sewing machine to decide the color, design, and decoration. These points can all be thought out in leisure moments, and when determined you have traveled just that far toward the completion of a successful garment.

When you see something about a dress that you like, or find an illustration showing features you believe you would like to use, cut out the picture and write down any thoughts you may have about the development of a similar garment. In this way, you make a definite impression on your memory, and as a result you will be able, at the desired time, to visualize the dress and compare its merits with your needs and thus reach a decision promptly.

I SHOULD never be able to read or to study if I waited for time in which to accomplish it. My interest makes me utilize every moment. I am sure that the little clippings which I gather from every source and with which I bulge my purse in readiness for a chance moment to read would be interesting to many of you. Recently I became particularly interested in a subject, procured the correspondence lessons regarding it, and set about to study for the information. I never found time at any one sitting to answer more than two questions. Often I would accomplish but one answer. I roughed it out on scrap paper and copied it later, and this plan gave me a review that was very advantageous.

WE CAN accomplish anything that we have the necessary determination for, study, growth, progress of every kind, if we use intelligently and opportunely every available moment.

I once wrote, "Impromptu visits with one's friends are as necessary to a development of the soul as religion itself," and impromptu visits with oneself about ambitions, desires, and accomplishments are a necessary stimulus to growth and progress.

I have always believed that there are three classes of people: Those who are

---

The practice of perseverance is the discipline of the noblest virtues. To run well, we must run to the end. It is not the fighting but the conquering that gives a hero his title to renown.

\* \* \*

All the performances of human art, at which we look with praise or wonder, are instances of the resistless force of perseverance; it is by this that the quarry becomes a pyramid, and that distant countries are united by canals. If a man was to compare the effect of a single stroke of a pickaxe, or of one impression of the spade, with the general design and last result, he would be overwhelmed with the sense of their disproportion; yet those petty operations, incessantly continued, in time surmount the greatest difficulties, and mountains are leveled and oceans bounded, by the slender force of human beings.

\* \* \*

Life affords no higher pleasure than that of surmounting difficulties, passing from one step of success to another, forming new wishes and seeing them gratified. He that labors in any great or laudable undertaking has his fatigues first supported by hope and afterwards rewarded by joy.

---

satisfied to have fate come and go at will with them. Another class who feel that all depends on them, that they are responsible, almost, for sun, rain, and stars. Then that class, to which I hope every one who reads this belongs, that class who know that there is a greater power than they, which is working always for their good, a power that by their appreciation of it can aid or retard.

Emerson says, "The starry crown of woman is in the power of her affection and sentiment and the infinite enlargements to which they lead." Every woman should be sentimental about her home and her tasks of homemaking and keeping, be they cleaning, cooking, or sewing, for it is through appreciation of these and the infinite privilege that home life affords that permanent affections are built. The influence of women is seen everywhere. It dominates home, school, church, and social life, and because of this the influence should be ever for good. Patience, kindness, truth, interest, cheeriness—all should be the daily companions of women who are privileged to mother homes, for the influences they evidence will be reflected in every avenue where their own have contact.

Being a woman is a privilege if one fully appreciates the responsibility and qualifies for the task—the task of keeping pace in every way with the growth and outreaching of the family interests, the task of acquiring skill meantime so that pride is felt for one's accomplishments rather than pity for the burdens one carries.

I KNOW a woman with a family who, at ten o'clock in the morning, fifteen years ago made a practice of saying that she did not have a thing to do all day. This woman is now saying she hasn't anything to do but worry because her daughters are ashamed of her. I personally know that the daughters are very unhappy because their mother has not progressed with them and other mothers they know. This mother casually looks at pictures in a magazine and is through with it. She has not read a book in many years, has no appreciation of pretty clothes, and no skill to make them for her children. Her home is not attractive, and yet she worries because her children are not proud of her.

As a child, Washington wrote in his copybook, "Labor to keep alive in your heart that little spark of celestial fire—conscience." I have always felt that this mother should have labored to be conscientious regarding her own time and what she could accomplish with it. She alone wasted a fortune in time and has had no happiness meanwhile, because happy hearts cannot stay with idle hands. To be happy inside, to grow in thought, to keep young, to be interesting, all of which are essentially success, you must fix your heart upon living every day, learn as much as you can, give out as much happiness and helpfulness as you can; fix your heart upon doing these things, and be enthusiastic about achieving them, remembering that enthusiasm, interest, and belief in oneself are the genius of sincere accomplishment and the very torch of victory.

Of belief in oneself, E. G. Lawrence says: "Belief founded on knowledge is the one means that leads to success; he who believes in himself because he knows himself capable, is destined to achieve what he sets out to accomplish."

# Making *Old* Hats *New*

### By MARY MAHON
### Department of Millinery

WITH the advent of warm weather and the vacation spirit in the air, a goodly share of thought must be given to the hat, because it may either bring out and top off the pleasing effects of one's pretty gowns and frocks or utterly ruin one's general appearance. The feeling that you are properly dressed on all occasions is a big factor in the true benefit that your vacation period is intended to bring, that is, thorough rest to the nervous system.

Some nerve specialists are advising a dress cure for the blues, claiming that a new hat is a greater stimulant than any tonic for nervous depression. I believe in the influence of color on the health and spirits, and the necessity for all women, especially business women, to make changes in their wardrobe frequently. This does not mean that they must be constantly buying new clothes; in fact, such a thing would be impossible, especially for those of limited means. But there are numerous other ways in which this change can be accomplished.

IN THE case of hats, remarkable results can be achieved by touching them up a little, renovating them with a thorough steaming, adding a new flower or facing, or shaping them a little differently. And now is an opportune time to assemble all your hats for remodeling, for no matter how you decide to spend your vacation, whether you take a boat or a motor trip, or spend a few weeks at the seashore or quietly in the country, you will need several hats in order to feel properly dressed.

PROBABLY you have a sailor that, with a little retouching, can be made strictly up to the minute and will serve as a traveling hat. If your sailor is one of the dark, staple shades, a coat of glossy Colorite will brighten it up, and if you desire a little color, you might use a bias band of Persian silk draped in tight folds and finished at the right side in a tucked-under fold or by a loose end falling off the brim. Or a pretty brilliant band of Roman-stripe ribbon might be drawn around the crown and made to end in a tailored bow at the left side. As veils are an important hat accessory, the well-dressed woman is seldom seen without one, so a net veil with a scroll design or an entire lace veil draped over the sailor and falling loosely to the shoulders will give just the proper effect to a smart Eton suit or topcoat.

PERHAPS, away back in January, when the first straw hats appeared, you purchased a Chin Chin turban of liséré or Milan that gave splendid service during the spring, but now it appears somewhat heavy and its flowers faded. In order to give it a new touch, why not decide to bring out the transparent effect so popular at this particular time and make it feel at home with the new transparent hats? If you desire the entire brim transparent, rip off the original brim to about 1½ inches from the head-size. Then attach four stay wires to a wire at the head-size, shape them out and up, and apply the edge wire. This edge wire can be wound with strips of maline to give it an even, round finish and to provide an edge to which the hair braid can be sewed. Purchase pyroxylin braid 1 inch wide and sew a row on the edge wire and allow it to extend beyond this. Sew the next row to this one and continue in this manner in to the head-size. For trimming, combine some new flowers with strands of different colored ostrich and a soft, fluffy touch will be produced.

ANOTHER idea for this same hat consists in attaching one row of horsehair braid on the edge of the brim, and, beginning at the base of the crown, outlining the entire crown with hair braid. Be careful not to take any stitches through the crown in sewing the braid together. After the entire crown is covered, hold it over a steaming teakettle and allow the steam to penetrate every part of it, in order to conform the shape of the hair braid to the straw crown. Then, from the inside, rip the straw crown off about ½ inch from the head-size, and you have a transparent crown and edge. Such a hat requires very little trimming, a band of narrow moiré ribbon drawn around the crown with a bow at the back and a pretty jet pin stuck

through the outside of the brim in the direct front usually being sufficient. A silk tassel attached to the under-brim at the right side back will give a smart effect.

FOR the last few years, the sports hat has taken a decided hold on milady's heart and has proved to be a necessary part of a complete wardrobe. This year it is reappearing in countless ways, but chiefly in the form of body, or large flat, hats, made of yedda and barnyard straws in various colors. They are especially appealing when they match one's sweater. Many of them are worn large and floppy as they come, with just a tight band and a bow at the side. Others are cut at the edge and wired to give a little rolled effect in the front, and then bound with narrow faille ribbon of contrasting color or solidly embroidered with raffia and wool. Still others are trimmed with organdie, voile, or any other cotton fabric used for summer frocks.

In many cases, the entire hat is made of one of these fabrics, but organdie seems to predominate. Sometimes, a flat straw braid is used for the facing on a netine frame and an accordion-plaited ruffle of organdie for the top brim, this being placed so as to extend out over the edge about 1 inch. The crown may be made in the soft tam or sectional effect. The trimming is very simple, such as a sash of the organdie embroidered in many bright colors and tied around the crown with a soft bow at the back. In many instances, the most pleasing effect imaginable is produced by appliquéing velvet flowers in daring colors on white or pastel organdie hats.

In accordance with the present popularity of the ciré effect, many of the sports hats have crowns of ciré ribbon, which is very soft and thin and looks like leather, and brims of plain or brocaded duvetyn in both the staple and the bright colors. For others, duvetyn makes the upper brim and jockey crowns, that is, crowns made in four or five pieces, and white tagal or hemp, the facing. To wear with such hats, various kinds of duvetyn scarfs and jackets have been designed. One popular sleeveless jacket in a pastel shade had its edge buttonholed and its belt and pockets embroidered in white angora. Duvetyn scarfs are embroidered and fringed with angora.

IN CASE you have a white straw hat that is burnt with the sun, you can cover the entire top of your hat with white organdie or any cotton fabric that will match your frock. Bind the edge with black oilcloth and buttonhole-stitch white angora over the black binding. A 3-inch band of black oilcloth embroidered in a floral design with white angora across the front will give you a decidedly new study in black and white when drawn around the crown and finished with a bow at the side or back.

# Vacation Needs Anticipated

By ALWILDA FELLOWS
Department of Dressmaking

FOR some reason or other the planning and making of clothes for special occasions generally proves much more interesting than any attention given to garments that must be provided for usual needs. And, as a rule, such garments are very successful, in spite of the fact that a great deal of time is seldom spent on them. Perhaps this is because of the enthusiasm and eager anticipation that go with each stitch put into a frock or wardrobe intended for a joyous event; this very enthusiasm is an element necessary to successful dressmaking and to satisfaction, for when one is disinterested or treats a subject in a halfhearted or matter-of-fact way, nothing unusual is apt to come out of one's work. On the other hand, just a spark of wholehearted effort can produce wonders.

Not to be counted as the least of the events that act as a spur to dressmaking endeavors, summer vacation time will soon be making its needs keenly felt.

WHEN vacation clothes are brought into consideration, the first sort of costume that comes to the minds of those fond of outdoor life is the sports dress. At one time we depended almost entirely on the middy blouse and separate skirt of rather coarse, ordinary weaves for sports wear. How different now, when the variety of styles and materials is so great that it tends to rival the selection that is offered for street, afternoon, or evening dresses. In fact, it is becoming rather difficult to draw a distinct dividing line between styles and materials suitable for sports and those used for street and afternoon wear. Therefore, if a sports dress is carefully selected, a point may be stretched, when necessary, and the sports dress made to serve for another occasion.

MATERIAL is an important consideration when a double-service dress is required, but even greater care should be given to the selection of a style. The lines of the dress must be loose, the skirt of ample width, and the whole suggestive of coolness and comfort; yet the style should be in conservative accordance with Fashion's dictates in regard to street or afternoon costumes.

The problem of developing a style suggestive of all these features is quite successfully solved in Le Costume Royal design 5884, which is shown at the left in the center illustration. This is made of heavy silk crêpe in putty color and depends on no contrasting color or material for trimming, as the bindings and buttons are of self-fabric. The suggestion of a middy leads one to assume that this is its modernized version.

The spring Home pattern book shows a similar blouse design 2534, the principal difference being the finish at the neck line, which is band in the Home design.

THE skirt of such a style may be of straight lengths of material pressed in rather wide knife plaits by hand or in accordion or narrow knife steam plaiting.

Variations of this style may be made by using two kinds of material, such as natural-colored pongee for the blouse and plain rose, blue, brown, or green or figured pongee for the skirt, the collar, and the trimming bands on the elbow-length sleeves. Plain and plaid ginghams or two colors of linen also offer possibilities.

If desired only for an afternoon dress, the style would be lovely developed in blue or black satin with an embroidery design placed just above the low waist line.

THE typical summer-afternoon frock is practically indispensable. Many of this season's models, especially those of organdie, consist almost entirely of ruffles. Such styles, however, are rather trying unless one is quite youthful and slender and, besides, they consume a great deal of time in laundering. If a more conservative model is desired, the dress may be made similar to the illustration at the right. It is impossible to obtain a pattern that duplicates this design, but the construction of the dress is so very simple that it may be easily made without a special pattern.

The skirt consists of two straight pieces of material sufficiently long to form the very wide hem that is illustrated. A matching feature is introduced by applying a straight band of material on the wrong side in the center of the skirt. Hemstitching is used to secure the applied band, the skirt hem, the cuff band to the sleeve, and the hem in the vestee.

The waist may be cut with a plain pattern, kimono sleeves, if preferred, and the collar developed with the use of a true bias strip of material carefully adjusted to form the rolled effect and left open at the back.

Made of organdie in a pastel color, with fine lace as a trimming, and picoted or double-faced ribbon of self-color or contrasting color for the finish at the waist line, this style would be lovely. If made of a rather bright color, however, the dress would be more attractive without the lace, and, as a substitute, the collar and cuffs bound with self-material in scallop effect.

Voile, lawn, batiste, Georgette crêpe, and any plain-colored sheer materials are suitable for this style. Developed in white, it would serve very well for graduation.

DURING the past few years, a great deal of attention has been directed toward beach and bathing costumes. This first type of costume is really non-essential and therefore deserves no consideration from the practical girl or woman. Bathing suits, however, should be chosen with care and the keenest discrimination employed in regard to style and fabric.

Many of the features considered essential for a sports costume may be applied in the development of a bathing suit. Such a suit should, by all means, be sufficiently loose to provide ample freedom in swimming, but it should not have excessive fulness that would prove cumbersome. The style should be modest, but, even so, it may be decidedly smart and attractive.

A variety of materials ranging from cottons, through woolens, to silk are being featured in bathing costumes. Wool is preferred by the majority of persons, however, because of its warmth. Wool jersey is an especially desirable material for this purpose. Brilliantine is another fabric that is very satisfactory.

Elite design 4209D, illustrated at the lower right, is given as an example of a practical, attractive bathing costume. The trimming is of military braid arranged on the skirt in border effect. Bands of bright contrasting color may be substituted if desired. In this case, a tie of the same color would add a pleasing touch to the costume.

# The Great American Dessert—*Pie*

By LAURA MacFARLANE
Editorial Department

WHEN we come to look into the matter of food so far as countries are concerned, we find that the majority of them have some national dishes. In America, we seem to have fewer of these than most countries, probably because of the nature of our population, but of those attributed to us, pie certainly takes leading rank. Indeed, America may be said to be the land

Where girls are wooed for the tarts they make,
Where women are loved for the pies they bake,
And the husbandman prays when he comes to die
He will go to heaven where all is pie.

Yes, pie is essentially a man's dessert. One could hunt for many a day and not be able, I'm sure, to find a man who would not accord pastry in its various forms the first place in the long list of desserts that fill the average cook book. Consequently, it behooves the American housewife to learn the secrets of pastry-making and to become proficient, through practice, in the art of making pies that will not only appeal to the members of her household, but perpetuate her well-earned fame for light, flaky pastry.

IN THIS phase of cookery, as in all others, there are certain principles that must be understood if the best results would be had. Chief among these is the fact that all the ingredients should be as cold as possible. Ice water is found most satisfactory and both the flour and the fat will work up better if they are very cold.

Pastry flour, which is made from winter wheat and which contains less gluten and therefore lacks the gummy consistency of bread flour, is the most desirable. A solid fat is the best shortening. Lard has always been a particular favorite, but for ordinary purposes, various combinations of fat of both animal and vegetable origin prove good substitutes.

Pastry should be baked as quickly as possible. The correct temperature for most pastry is from 500 to 600 degrees, which is the hottest oven ever used for food. When the filling does not require so much baking as the crust, as in custard pie, the crust should be partly baked before the filling is added. On the other hand, pies containing certain kinds of filling must be baked slowly. The baking may be begun in a very hot oven and the heat then gradually reduced until the filling is cooked.

The steam that forms in the baking of a two-crust pie must have an outlet, or the crust will be pushed up and the appearance of the pie spoiled. Usually, the openings in the design on the top crust are sufficient, but in the case of a very juicy pie, a funnel may be made out of a small piece of paper and then inserted into one of the openings in the top crust.

THERE are, of course, numerous kinds of pastry, but the ones that are made most frequently are plain pastry, in which the fat is worked in all at once and the entire mass then rolled out, and rolled pastry, which we shall term quality paste and in which part of the shortening is cut in and the remainder rolled into the dough. This is usually made when an especially flaky crust is desired. These pastes are made as follows:

### PLAIN PASTRY

| | |
|---|---|
| 1½ c. flour | ½ c. shortening |
| ½ tsp. salt | ¼ to ⅓ c. water |

With the ingredients collected and the utensils conveniently placed, sift the flour with the salt into the mixing bowl and cut in the fat with the aid of two knives until the pieces are about the size of a small pea. Then heap the particles up in the center of the bowl, make a hole in the mixture, and pour the water into this in a thin stream, stirring the mixture all the time with a knife or a spatula. Gather into a mass and place enough to cover a pie pan on a floured board. With a light, careful motion of a very cold rolling pin, roll until about ⅛ inch thick, keeping the piece as nearly round as possible. Cover a pie pan and trim the edge evenly by running a knife around it. For a two-crust pie, roll out the remainder of the pastry and have it ready to apply after the filling has been added.

### QUALITY PASTE

| | |
|---|---|
| 2 c. flour | ⅓ to ½ c. water |
| ¼ tsp. salt | ½ c. butter |
| ¼ c. lard | |

Sift the flour and salt into a mixing bowl, add the lard, and chop very fine. Work in enough water to make a stiff dough. Roll in a rectangular form, spread the butter evenly over the paste, and fold so as to form three layers. Turn half way round and roll out so as to make a rectangle in the opposite direction. Fold, turn, and roll in this way four times, handling the rolling pin and paste as lightly as possible. Use to cover a pan and bake in a quick oven.

THE universal favorite among pies is unquestionably apple pie. And what makes a more delicious ending to a good meal, whether it is a light one or a heavy one, than pie of this kind? It is especially appealing when served with ice cream as pie à la mode. A small square of cheese usually accompanies apple pie, or a little may be grated over the top.

### APPLE PIE

| | |
|---|---|
| 1 qt. apples | ½ tsp. cinnamon or |
| ½ to ¾ c. sugar | ¼ tsp. nutmeg |
| Salt | Lemon juice |

Peel the apples, cut them into pieces of the desired size, and heap them into a pan that has been covered with paste. Sprinkle with the sugar, salt, and cinnamon or nutmeg. Add 1 teaspoonful of lemon juice, and, if the apples seem dry, a few tablespoonfuls of water. Dot with butter, wet the edges of the under crust, and place the top crust in position. Bake in a hot oven about 45 minutes.

DURING the berry season, no dessert is so much in favor as huckleberry pie. Blackberries and raspberries may be used in the same way as huckleberries, so the following recipe has many possibilities.

### HUCKLEBERRY PIE

| | |
|---|---|
| 3 to 4 c. berries | 3 Tb. flour |
| ½ to ¾ c. sugar | Pinch of salt |

Look the berries over carefully and remove any spoiled ones, leaves, and stems. Wash thoroughly and fill the lower crust. Add the sugar mixed with the flour and salt. Cover with the top crust and bake for 30 minutes in a moderately hot oven.

AMONG one-crust pies, and there are many of these, pineapple pie seems to be taking the lead. So when you want a change from lemon pie, which has so long held sway, just try the following recipe:

### PINEAPPLE PIE

| | |
|---|---|
| ½ c. corn starch | ⅔ c. pineapple juice |
| 1 c. sugar | 2 Tb. lemon juice |
| ¼ tsp. salt | 1 c. shredded or finely |
| 1½ c. water | chopped pineapple |
| 1 egg | |

Mix the corn starch, sugar, and salt, add to the boiling water, and cook until thick. Separate the egg, beat the yolk, and add to the pineapple and lemon juice. Stir this into the corn-starch mixture, remove from the heat, and add the pineapple. Pour into a baked crust, cover with a meringue made of the egg white, and bake in a moderate oven until delicately browned.

For such pies, the meringue is made by beating the chilled egg whites until they are almost stiff and then adding 1 tablespoonful of confectioner's sugar for each egg white. The sugar should be added slowly and the beating continued until all is incorporated. A little vanilla or lemon juice is often added for flavoring.

IF A pie that will please old and young alike is desired, custard pie should be made. And now that eggs can be used with a little more freedom, we can indulge ourselves by having pie of this kind more frequently. It is very much improved by the addition of fresh coconut, but this may be omitted from the recipe as given if it is not available.

### COCONUT-CUSTARD PIE

| | |
|---|---|
| 3 eggs | 1 c. shredded coconut |
| 3 c. milk | ¼ tsp. salt |
| ¾ c. sugar | 1 tsp. vanilla |

Beat the eggs slightly and add the milk, sugar, coconut, salt, and vanilla. Partly bake the crust, pour in the custard, place in a moderate oven, and bake until a knife will come out clean when inserted.

# Calico Frocks

ALONG with the overall fad for men comes a great wave of fashion for calico. It seems that there is a disagreement as to the virtue of all our men folk adopting overalls, many saying that it will increase the price of cotton, burden the overall manufacturers, and not bring about a definite solution of the high clothing prices that prevail. But there can be no argument regarding the true economy of calico frocks. They are delightful to wear and easy to launder; besides, the material is easily adaptable to fashion's fancies. This season there are some truly smart calico frocks made with as much cleverness as one could evidence with dainty organdie, voile, or gingham, and they cost only about one-half the price of dresses of the other materials.

MOST of the calico frocks are trimmed in lawn, organdie, or voile. For instance, one with a light-tan ground had a plain-tan organdie collar, cuffs, pocket, and sash, and was delightfully crisp and smart. The same mode of trimming could be used for calico with blue and pink grounds. Many calico frocks carry pockets, short sleeves, a comfy summer neck line, and a definite waist-line finish, the latter in either sash or belt effect. Rick-rack braid makes an excellent trimming for calico dresses.

Styles 2105, 2217, 2361, 2026, 2137, and 2140 in the *Butterick Summer Quarterly,* 9461, 9109, 9413, and 9257 in the *McCall Quarterly,* and 8374, 8726, 8700, 8287, 8213, and 8166 in the *Pictorial Review Quarterly* would be very pretty made up in calico, especially if daintily trimmed with suitable colored or white material. A study of any of the fashion books or magazines for summer will show many suitable styles.

CALICO, because of the rather lowly position it has held since the time of our grandmothers, cannot rely on its weave and texture alone to excite interest or admiration. Trimming of an unusual nature contributes much to the success of a calico frock, but of equal importance are the neatness and care exercised in making it.

In almost any design suitable for calico, French seams may be used throughout. The firmness of the weave of this fabric makes it possible to use very narrow seams that do not prove cumbersome nor conspicuous. A very essential precaution to take in making narrow French seams is to trim the seam unusually close to the first stitching, so that none of the frayed ends will be discernible on the right side.

Machine stitching may be used more generally than in the development of silk dresses. For instance, as a rule, hems may be stitched rather than secured by hand, and stitching may also be employed for the application of trimming of various kinds.

Pearl, vegetable, or bone buttons are noted on many calico frocks, but the most attractive buttons are those covered with the trimming material and embroidered in some odd manner. In this case, the use of bone button molds is essential, for wooden molds are not satisfactory for use on garments requiring frequent laundering.

THE expense of making calico frocks is not great and the time required to make them is scarcely a consideration, so why not make at least one for yourself, your sister, or your neighbor, if only to see how pretty it is and to prove that you can make a smart frock in a few hours?

The "dollar-an-hour" slogan for housewives surely puts a new emphasis on time that has not been properly valued before; but it is easy to prove the slogan true if one sets out with real determination to make every spare hour yield a dollar's worth of accomplishment.

# Woman's Institute *Question-Box*

## Handling Knitted Fabrics

How do you handle Jersey and tricolette as to cutting, fitting, and pressing? How do you keep the hem from appearing gathered when it is sewed? How may I wash white wool Jersey? How dry it? How press it?        D. L. T.

Of primary importance in the planning of garments to be cut from knitted fabrics is the selection of a rather simple design, one having comparatively straight lines and very few seams. Cut the fabric in the usual manner, with long, even strokes, first making sure that the pattern pieces are laid on the correct grain of the material. Immediately after cutting and before doing any pinning or basting, stitch ¼ inch inside of each cut edge in order to catch the threads of the material and prevent them from fraying while the garment is being made.

In fitting, make sure that no portion of the garment is made so tight that it will have a tendency to stretch.

Press each stage of the work very carefully, following the general instructions for pressing woolen materials when doing this, but taking the added precaution of pressing so far as possible in the direction of the warp threads.

To prevent a gathered or drawn appearance in the hem, do not turn the edge under. Secure it with rather loose catch-stitches taken close together and made barely discernible on the right side. If you prefer, you may bind the hem edge with very soft silk and catch this with fine, loose hemming-stitches.

In order to wash white wool Jersey, first prepare a soap jelly of some pure white soap, or use soap flakes with lukewarm water. After the soap is mixed with the water, place the garment in the water and let it stand for ¼ or ½ hour. This will loosen most of the dirt. Then, in order to make the garment thoroughly clean, squeeze it gently through the hands and, if necessary, rub the decidedly soiled spots between the hands. Rinse immediately in plenty of clean lukewarm water.

Dry the garment as quickly as possible, but rather than hang it up, lay it on a smooth surface. This will prevent stretching. Press on the wrong side before the material is thoroughly dry. If necessary to do any pressing on the right side, first place a light-weight cloth over the material.

## Merchandise and Supplies

For the past few months we have been enclosing in INSPIRATION a price list of merchandise and supplies that we have to offer our students. It is omitted this month because of the serious shortage of print paper. Those who wish to make purchases from our Merchandise Service Department may be governed by the price list they received last month. New students who have not received a price list may have one on request. Our sampler materials should appeal to new students. Sampler materials for Essential Stitches and Seams, Part 1, may be had for 25 cents; for Part 2, 50 cents; for Millinery Stitches, 40 cents; for Embroidery Stitches, Parts 1 and 2, 30 cents.

## Want to Get Acquainted?

The following Institute students desire to become acquainted with other Institute students residing in their localities:

St. Paul, Minn. ............................... G. B.
Pittsburgh, Pa. ........................... T. E. H. K.
Reynoldsville, Pa. ........................... E. D.
Charles City, Iowa ........................... C. S.
Gas City, Ind. ............................... C. F. F.
Hartington, Neb. ........................... H. M. E.
Pontiac, Mich. ............................... H. W.
Seattle, Wash. ............................... F. K.
Evanston, Ill. ............................... L. J.
Apple River, Ill. ........................... L. M. G.
Oakland, Calif. ............................... C. C.
Omaha, Neb. ............................... C. A. C.
Cisco, Ill., or Cerro Gordo, Ill. ............ G. E.
Jacksonville, Fla. ........................... J. E. G.
Lewisville, Ark. ........................... R. C. P.
Covina, Calif. ............................... B. F. T.
East Boston, Mass. ........................... M. H.
Sioux City, Iowa ........................... H. W.
Corvallis, Ore. ........................... F. W. P.
Watkins, Minn. ............................... G. M.

I should like to become acquainted with some girl about twenty years of age, taking the Dressmaking and Tailoring Course in Sioux Falls, S. Dak.        G. M.

I should like to become acquainted with some Institute students about 18 years of age, who live in Wisconsin or some neighboring states. R. H.

I should like to become acquainted or to correspond with some Institute students about 15 years of age who are taking the Complete Dressmaking Course.        C. McK.

I should like to obtain work with a Woman's Institute student in business in Calgary or Edmonton, Canada.        P. V. K.

If other Woman's Institute students would like to get in touch with the inquiring students, we shall be glad to supply the addresses.

# Our Students' *Own Page*

## "Facing the Future Without Worry"

What a volume of meaning is conveyed by those few words. And yet that is exactly what hundreds of our members are doing today, secure in the realization that, come what may, in the way of financial reverses or loss of support, they have, in their training in Dressmaking or Millinery, the ability to support themselves and their little ones in comfort. Mrs. Edwin H. Dinzey, who lives away up in Alberta, Canada, expressed this thought very well and we are going to give it to you in her own words:

I consider it was the luckiest day in my life when I answered an advertisement in one of the magazines, and decided to take your Dressmaking Course. Thanks to the confidence you inspire in your students, I can face the future without worry, even though I must support my four-year-old son and myself.

## Method and System in the Home

What might be called an indirect result of the mental exercise and training one gets from a systematic Course in Dressmaking is referred to in a letter we recently received from Mrs. R. P. Mase, one of our enthusiastic Pittsburgh members. There is no doubt that the work they do on their Courses has enabled many women to "find themselves," figuratively speaking. It has opened their eyes to what can be accomplished through the careful and systematic use of one's time. Mrs. Mase writes:

I consider your Dressmaking Course the best course of study I have ever received and I am a college graduate. Everything is so excellent that I haven't had one bit of trouble. There is a lot of satisfaction in knowing there isn't a hole to be darned in the house, that everything is in its right place, methodically put away, clean and whole! Your Course has done that for me and I am only on my sixth lesson.

## Sold Two Hundred Hats Last Season

It is always a satisfaction to receive letters of appreciation from graduates, women who, after completing the entire Course, are able to say "You have done everything that you promised you would do," or, as nearly every graduate says it one way or another, "I have enjoyed the lessons so much that I am sorry they are finished." You will probably enjoy reading the following letter from Mrs. M. Kircher, one of our recent Millinery graduates from Adrian, Minn. Mrs. Kircher says:

I am today finishing my last lesson. First of all I will express my heartfelt thanks to each and every one for the assistance they have rendered me. I know I shall be lonesome for my lessons for some

## Anniversary Winners

Our members will be interested to learn the outcome of our Fourth Anniversary Testimonial to Mrs. Picken. We are publishing the names of the Winners here, and in an early issue of INSPIRATION we hope to give a full account of our Anniversary Celebration and Cornerstone Laying for the handsome new building that will be the permanent home of the Institute. The winners are:

*Trips to Scranton*
Mrs. George H. Duker, Iowa City, Iowa
Mrs. Richard Spooner, Winchendon, Mass.
Mrs. Clara Coith Nelson, Greenleaf, Kans.
Mrs. Franklin Beecher, York, Pa.

*White Sewing Machine*
Mrs. J. C. Dodgson, Salt Lake City, Utah

*Wilson Electric Sewing Machine*
Mrs. J. L. Waldron, Oregon City, Utah

*Napanee Kitchen Cabinet*
Mrs. Frances Blunk Ford, Peoria, Ill.

*Course in Woman's Institute*
Mrs. A. S. Dickson, Beaver, Okla.

*Gold Bracelet Watch*
Mrs. Etta R. D. Piper, Altoona, Pa.

*Chest of Oneida Community Silver*
Mrs. O. E. Bevan, Clackamas, Ore.

*Martha Washington Sewing Companion*
Miss Edith Daniels, Dola, Ohio

The following members were tie for the next three Special Gifts, and each was offered her choice of a Dress Form, a Sanitary White Enamel Top Kitchen Table, and the Woman's Institute Five-Volume Library of Cookery:
Mrs. Elbert McCollum, Simsbury, Conn.
Mrs. Martin Rylander, Skanee, Mich.
Mrs. Art Schroll, Hutchinson, Kans.
Lenore Powell, Arcadia, Pa.
Mrs. M. A. Engel, Ridgewood, N. J.
Mrs. Mildred Daniels, Fredonia, Kans.
Mrs. Minnie L. Edward, Milan, Ga.
Mrs. Earl Hecker, Halliday, N. Dak.
Miss Florence Sielerman, Sperry, Iowa
Mrs. Mary O'Brien, Chicago, Ill.
Mrs. H. M. Hughes, Oil City, Pa.
Mary Kircher, Adrain, Minn.

time, as I was always anxiously looking for the next one to come, and studied with great pleasure. I will tell you a little about my millinery shop. I must say so far I have had good success, for a little place like this and two millinery stores. I sold nearly two hundred hats last season. This spring I hope to do still better, as this is only January and I am starting to sell my hats already. Now, they tell me that is doing fine.

## Wonders How Our Fees Can be So Low

Many of our members express surprise that our fees are so low as compared with the value of the service we render and the training we give. They do seem small when one thinks of the substantial savings a knowledge of Dressmaking or Millinery will enable one to make or the money such a training will qualify a woman to earn. Mrs. W. J. Cameron, of Belding, Mich., mentioned this point in a letter she wrote us recently. She said:

I cannot see why $65 used to look so big to me for the Course of Sewing I undertook, for now it seems such a trifle for all I have gained thus far; and yet there is so much more I have coming to me in my lessons. The Institute of Domestic Arts and Sciences is certainly a great help to the women of our country, and I am glad I chose this school when I was deciding on where to enroll.

## Commendation From Woman of Discriminating Taste

A little while ago we received the following interesting letter from Mrs. Grace Dunlap, of Medford, Mass., that we believe you will enjoy reading:

I must tell you of a very happy experience I had. Just before Christmas I made a very pretty dark-green broadcloth dress for a lady. A few weeks ago she met me at church and said: "Mrs. Dunlap, everybody is just crazy about this dress. (She had it on.) She said: "You know I work in Harvey's in Boston and you probably know that we cater to a very exclusive trade. I have many customers of the extremely wealthy people who have all they want and only the best. The other day I was waiting on a customer to whom I sell a great deal. She said, 'Would you mind telling me if you had that dress made which you have on?' I told her I did. 'Well,' she said, 'I have been looking at that dress. It is so perfect, so beautifully made, and so very artistic.' Then she added, 'I have been going to the finest tailors on Boylston Street here in Boston, and I have paid enormous prices, but I have never yet had anything made by them that would compare with that dress you have on. Would you be willing to tell me the name and address of your dressmaker?'"

This, of course, my customer was very glad to do. Now it really doesn't make a great deal of difference to me whether that lady comes out here to me or not. What I do value is the fact that my work was of sufficient beauty and quality to call forth admiration from a person who is used to patronizing exclusive tailors and modistes. My Course has meant everything to me and I consider my training to be priceless.

# Fashion Service

## SUPPLEMENT

Each Issue of *Vintage Notions Monthly* includes a *Fashion Service Supplement*. You will read about the fashion styles popular in the early twentieth century and receive a collectible fashion illustration to print and frame.

The students of the Woman's Institute would also receive a publication called *Fashion Service*. Where the *Inspiration* newsletter instructed them on all aspects of the domestic arts, not only sewing but also cooking, housekeeping, decorating, etc., *Fashion Service* was devoted entirely to giving current fashions with a key to their development.

*Fashion Service* prided itself on providing it's readers with reliable style information and the newest fashion forecasting. The publication wasn't just eye candy. The Institute stressed the importance of studying the fashions to benefit the sewer's understanding of dressmaking. To quote founder Mary Brooks Picken, "Once the principles of design...and of construction… are understood, beautiful garments will result. This publication comes to you as an aid to this desired goal. Read the text of every page and reason out the why of every illustration and description that your comprehension of designing and construction may be enlarged and your appreciation made more acute."

Today, these articles and illustrations give us a historically accurate view of what fashion really meant 100 years ago. Not only can we study these articles for an "of-the-time" style snapshot, but just as their students did, we can also learn to understand the principles of design and increase our sewing skills. In each issue, look for a collectible illustration in the back of the supplement!

# Springtime Fashions

"Three minutes more!" says an excited voice at the next table.

Dinner is over.

The waiters with their last trays of silver and crystal are hurrying out of the great hotel ballroom.

The orchestra is softly playing the "Spring Song."

Every inch of space in this beautiful room is filled with those whose foresight or influence has secured them precious tickets of admission. Even far into the dim recesses under the opposite balcony one sees women in the splendor of evening gowns, men in formal attire. Everywhere chairs have been shifted, and two thousand pairs of eyes are focused on the stage far up at the end. Through those gorgeous draperies at any moment now will appear the first model displaying what Fashion decrees shall be spring's dominant note in dress.

There is a breathless pause. A page appears bearing a silken banner with the name of the first exhibitor.

And then the draped folds are parted and a girl—all grace and beauty—slips out. She strolls twice back and forth across the stage, then descends the broad flight of stairs and steps out upon the elevated promenade that extends down through the center the full length of the great room. A battery of spotlights plays upon her.

"Dent de lion!" says a voice at the next table. "It is the new color."

"And the skirt is longer," says another, "or at least those side panels give the effect."

But already eyes are turning again to the stage, for another figure has appeared, in a dashing sports costume.

And following her comes another—and so for two hours passes the procession.

"What an exquisite shade of blue—periwinkle, they call it."

"And how many of the suits have a touch of red—why, there comes one all red—rouge red is the correct name."

And so one hears the comments springing from gay lips as observant eyes note the distinctive points of color and line in each new revelation as it emerges and passes in review.

For this is the first of the Spring Fashion Shows. Here the great designers—Lucille, Hickson, Thurn, Joseph, Francis, Gidding—display for the first time their interpretation of fashions of the new season.

What a fascination Fashion holds, and what an opportunity it brings to women to express beauty through dress!

Every woman everywhere should know the joy of Fashion's interest, for it is ceaseless in its change and infinite in its variety. It turns the wheels of trade, it stirs the imagination of the artist, but, most important of all to you, it shows new ways to express through becoming dress your own individuality.

More than half the delight of new clothes is in their planning and in the sure knowledge that they truly express the style intelligence of the hour. FASHION SERVICE brings you a correct interpretation of the mode and it aids you to show your own discrimination in determining what of the mode is right for you.

So, as you turn these pages, just make believe that you are at the Fashion Shows, that you are on Fifth Avenue, that you are in the smart shops there, that you are looking with your own eyes at the creations of the foremost designers. For FASHION SERVICE brings them to you actually and carefully so that the mode may be familiar, the color right, the material, the line, all as you would have them to express perfectly the Spring and Summer Fashions of 1922.

*S*IMPLE ELEGANCE, ever a delightful quality in a bridal gown, combines suggestions of both dignity and youthfulness in this lovely model of white crêpe-back satin. Skilful draping of the one-piece front secured at the left side with a pearl ornament makes this drapery singularly attractive because of the bloused effect it produces. The wide band of lace, which forms a bertha effect in front, extends over the shoulders and pleasingly offsets the court train.

The arrangement of the tulle veil is similar to the one of Princess Mary's choosing, but the band that secures it is ornamented with pearls to harmonize with the trimming of the dress.

Combining the fascinations of taffeta in an orange verging on tiger lily and the finest of cream-colored lace, the bridesmaid's costume in semifitted-basque and full-skirt effect does not spurn an abundance of trimming when it is applied in such an irresistibly youthful and picturesque manner as this. A soft-plaited insert of cream-colored chiffon provides a background for the lace cascades that are used with unusual effect in the front of the skirt. The ribbon that encircles the bodice is of slightly darker tone than the taffeta, as are the roses that nestle in several sprays of soft, green foliage.

By comparison with the bridesmaid frock, the gown intended for a maid of honor or matron of honor bears added dignity. Its contrast in color, as well as in line, is very pleasing, for it is of deep mauve taffeta combined with cream lace and bloused with a self-colored ribbon sash to which are attached flowers of varied hue for a front waist-line finish. The sleeves are slashed to reveal almost the full length of the arm.

# Chemise Dress

Perhaps it was the beauty and utility of the sports clothes of a year ago, together with the popular favor accorded them, that inspired Fashion to make this a season in which the sports influence is the dominating note. Again, it may have been the more recent inspiration of the newest fabrics or the vivid colors that almost invariably suggest the great out-of-doors as a fitting background for them. It is enough, however, that a season of sports apparel is here and the eagerness and delight with which sports models have already been accepted are an indication that Fashion did not err in her decision to feature them.

Dresses of sports design are almost invariably of the chemise type, which is favored because of its simplicity and its loose, comfortable lines. The chemise type is by no means restricted to sports models, though, for it is found in the very dressiest costumes as well. In fact, although the chemise dress has been in favor so long, its possibilities today seem more varied than ever, for it may be used not only as a straight-hanging costume, but also as a blouse dress with waist line of any depth, a casing being applied at the point where the waist line is desired.

Of no less interest than the sports influence of this season are the capes, which have already attained a surprising amount of prestige. Not just one cape for one wardrobe is evident, but a cape to add smartness to the sports dress, one to complete the tailored suit, one to top the separate coat, one to adorn the after-noon frock, and one, but in this case of the filmiest of fabrics, to add grace and airiness to the evening gown. Many of these are in abbreviated effect and attached to the costume, in direct contrast to the long and full cover-all cape that is used as a wrap. But many more are of medium size, made separate from the costume, and worn when a little protection is needed.

Many of Fashion's fondest ambitions are realized in this costume, for besides its cape, which may be omitted if just the simple dress is desired, the vogue for white is recognized in the principal dress fabric, which is Canton crêpe, and homage is paid to the newest color, dent de lion, a yellow taken from the dandelion, in the trimming and the cape, which are of Roshanara crêpe. The oval buttons are of white bone.

The dress is a simple, practical style that suggests development in light or dark colors in materials such as jersey, tweed, tricotine, crêpe-knit, linen, ratiné, and gingham, the material deciding whether the dress shall be a sports or a street model.

*Material and Pattern Requirements.*—For the average figure, provide about 3 yards of material 32 to 40 inches wide, with 2½ yards of contrasting fabric for the dress and the cape. With the cape omitted, ¾ yard of trimming will be sufficient.

A one-piece kimono dress pattern is needed for cutting out the dress. If this does not have a vest portion of the kind illustrated, mark the outline in the development of a muslin model and trace this on paper to form a separate vest pattern.

A pattern is not really necessary for the cape, as this consists merely of a straight piece of material.

*Cutting.*—In cutting out the dress, do not cut away the center-front portion under the vest section. Rather, let it extend to the neck line and do not slash it for the opening until after the piece for the vest is applied.

For the cape, cut a straight piece about 1½ yards long and from 24 to 30 inches wide, according to the length you desire the cape. From the lengthwise piece that is left, cut a strip for the tie ends, making this 3½ inches wide and 1½ yards long, and another strip for the skirt trimming, making this 2 or 2½ inches wide and a trifle longer than the width of the skirt.

The "fence" collar of the cape consists of merely a double straight fold. For this, cut a crosswise strip about 13 inches wide and 22 to 26 inches long, according to the size you desire at the neck. Cut the vest and belt, also, crosswise of the fabric, cutting the belt about 3 inches wide and 8 inches longer than the waist measurement.

*Making the Dress.*—Apply the vest portion before sewing the under-arm seams, proceeding as you would in applying a facing strip for the center-front opening of a middy, but bringing the facing, or vest, to the right side. Turn under the outer edges of the vest and slip-stitch or stitch them in position.

Next, baste the under-arm seams and also the shoulder seams, if provision has been made for them, and try the dress on to observe what fitting is necessary. Finish the seams by pressing them open and overcasting the edges, with the exception of the seam that joins the sleeves to the dress; press these seam edges together back on the sleeve portion and overcast the edges.

Finish the sleeve edges with picoting, binding, or facing, according to the nature of the material.

Make the collar double and join it by stitching the under edge to the neck line first and then turning the other edge over this and securing it with whipping-stitches.

It will be necessary to apply a fly portion to the slashed opening. Cut this straight and of a double thickness 1½ inches wide. Place this so that the raw edges extend under the right edge of the slash and the fold will extend under the left edge when the dress is closed. Then secure it to the right edge with very close slip-stitches and overcast the raw edges.

After turning the hem, apply the trimming band at the lower edge as a facing turned to the right side.

Make the belt by folding the strip lengthwise through the center, stitching the raw seam edges together, and then turning it right side out and finishing the ends with an ornamental buckle or with buttons like those used for the dress.

If you wish pockets, make them in stand effect, being guided by the instructions in your lessons.

*Making the Cape.*—If the cape has been cut so that the selvage is along the lower edge and this selvage is not stamped nor of different texture from the material, you may leave this for a finish and simply hem the ends or front edges. Otherwise, have the edges picoted, or bind, face, or hem them, according to the nature of the fabric.

Make the collar double, shaping the upper half of the ends as shown. Then gather the neck edge of the cape, and apply the collar to this edge as you would apply a binding; that is, first stitch one edge to the gathered portion and then turn under the other edge and whip it down just beyond the stitching first made. Then fold the upper half of the collar down over the other half. Make the tie ends as suggested for making the belt of the dress and slip them through eyelets worked in the collar.

---

## Skirts Are Longer

"Is this to be another season when rumors of longer skirts will not materialize?" To this oft-repeated question, the answer is that already the longer skirt is being adopted and that by fall the extremely short skirt will be as a bell tinkling in the distance.

Skirt lengths vary with the style and purpose of the garment. Many evening models are of ankle length, afternoon dresses generally extend to within 8 or 9 inches of the floor, and street models to 9 or 10 inches. Sports models are reluctant to give up the comfort and smartness of the shorter lengths, and in these the abbreviated skirt is still in excellent standing, provided it does not verge on the knee-length styles that are so fast disappearing from view.

---

Model 1

# Variations of Chemise Dress

**Model 1A.**—Some colors do not seem at all reluctant to reveal their full beauty, even when used in the most ordinary of fabrics. Others—and periwinkle blue is one of the foremost of this class—are apparently so aristocratic by nature that under no consideration can they be persuaded to lend their complete charm to a fabric that does not correspond with their ideas of distinctiveness. One can hardly refrain from sympathizing with this viewpoint when periwinkle is observed in its preferred habitat, that is, in the silks of soft and lustrous weave, for here its subtle and delightful shading from blue to violet hues achieves a real triumph.

The simplicity of this design permits the fabric, which is of periwinkle Roshanara crêpe, to take credit for a great deal of the success of the costume. And yet, the double bands of white crêpe de Chine and the profusion of pearl buttons that accentuate the long lines contribute much to the attractiveness of the model.

The manner in which the flared sleeves are gathered into the portion of the trimming band that extends lengthwise in the sleeves is rather novel.

Crêpe de Chine forms the collar and the loose belt, which is in simple tailored style and is secured with a pearl buckle at the center front.

This model is an excellent one for cotton fabrics, such as those in éponge weave, chambray, and plain and checked gingham, and also very good for linen.

For the average figure, 3½ yards of material 40 inches wide, 1½ yards of contrasting fabric, and 7½ dozen buttons are required for this model.

For cutting out this costume, use a one-piece dress pattern having full-length front and back panel effects and a sleeve that fits into a rather close armhole but is flared toward the lower edge.

**Model 1B.**—If one delights in an unusual combination of fabrics, this model fashioned of rust-colored crêpe de Chine and beige ratiné or Fishermaid, a material woven in imitation of fish netting, is sure to find immediate favor. If one's taste is a trifle more conservative, one kind of material, such as crêpe de Chine, crêpe knit, linen, ratiné, or even voile in two harmonizing colors would certainly make its appeal.

As illustrated, the embroidery is a very simple design developed in darning-stitch, with heavy rust-colored and beige floss. An enlarged detail of the embroidery is shown at the bottom of the page of illustrations.

The sash of crêpe de Chine is extended through rings covered by means of a simple crochet-stitch with yarn like that used for the embroidery.

Of the material of lighter color, 2½ yards 36 inches wide is required, with 2¼ yards of the darker color and 3 skeins of floss.

You will probably find it difficult to obtain a pattern having seam lines that duplicate those of the model, but if you procure a plain-kimono dress pattern in straight-line effect with a seam at the hip line or a little above it, you will be able to mark the other seam lines on a muslin model and afterwards cut on the marked lines to form the various pattern sections. The panels, which are attached at the hip line and extended below the skirt hem, are simply straight pieces of material.

An elastic drawn through a casing placed at a low waist line makes the blouse effect possible. If the neck is not cut sufficiently deep to permit the dress to be slipped over the head, you may make a short opening from the neck along the left-side seam line and finish this with narrow facing.

**Model 1C.**—When Fashion introduces a seam line that is a bit trying for the majority of types, and this is true of the line used this season to suggest a deep yoke effect in a kimono blouse, the very best thing to do is to break the severity of this seam line and make it generally more becoming. Such a treatment is very successfully carried out by the straight plaited sections that extend from horizontal slashes 2 or 3 inches above the seam line at the side front and side back of this charming model of crêpe de Chine in plain white and figured rose and white. A similar arrangement is noted in the sleeve, also. The girdle of rose-colored ribbon is finished with a rosette made of cut ends of the ribbon in modified star effect, from which hang loops and long ends of ribbon.

Figured and plain voile or any of the other printed cotton fabrics of light-weight weave in combination with a plain color suggest other possibilities for this design. If you prefer, you may substitute machine hemstitching or braid in imitation of fagoting for the fagoted seam lines.

Supply 5 yards of 40-inch fabric, ¾ yard of contrasting material, and 4½ yards of ribbon for developing this design for the average figure.

This dress, also, though of the chemise type, has an elastic drawn through a low waist-line casing to give a bloused effect.

**Model 1D.**—White Kasha cloth, the new woolen fabric that has already met with so much favor, makes a charming background for the yarn embroidery of jade and black that transforms this erstwhile plain chemise model into a design of striking individuality. How simply and rapidly the embroidery can be developed is shown by the enlarged detail at the right, outlining- and darning-stitches being the only ones required for it, as the illustration shows.

Fringe of wool matching that used for the embroidery finishes the lower edge of the skirt. This feature is one that is noted on a great many spring models.

Another very interesting feature of this dress is the sharp contrast afforded by the jade crêpe de Chine, which provides the peasant sleeves, the collar, and the vestee.

Average requirements for this model include 2½ yards of 54-inch fabric and 1¼ yards of contrasting material 40 inches wide, with 8 small skeins of yarn.

To form the inverted plaits at the sides of this dress, in cutting, make an extension of 2½ inches on the back edge of the under-arm seam from the waist line to the lower edge and an extension of 6½ inches on the front edge and mark-stitch along the original side seams as a guide for turning the plaits. Then, in making the dress, after stitching ½-inch seams in the skirt, instead of pressing them open, fold the plaits under on the mark-stitched lines and press them so that the plaits are of equal depth; this will bring the seam at the back inside edge of the plait.

**Model 1E.**—Designers are not at all hesitant about using the brightest and warmest colors for spring frocks, as noted in this model of Roshanara crêpe of a red that verges on flame color. Detracting somewhat from the vividness, white crêpe de Chine forms the upper sleeve portion, the collar, and the vest. But, again, a sprinkling of the flame color is shown on the sleeves, where chenille dots, which are applied in the form of French knots and placed at regular intervals, form an all-over effect.

This design is another that would be very effective developed in cotton or linen fabrics. In flame-colored linen combined with tissue having a white background and a small plaid of flame color or in white Swiss having a flame-colored dot, the model would be very smart, although other colors and combinations may also be used to excellent advantage.

About 3 yards of material 36 inches wide with ¾ yard of contrasting fabric is required for the average figure.

If the left side of the vest of this design is supplied with snap fasteners rather than secured to the dress, it will be possible to slip the dress over the head with ease.

1A

1B

1C

1D

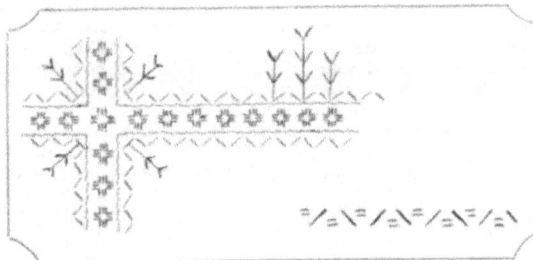

1E

# Blouse Dress

One particular difference between the present type of blouse dress and the blouse dress of last season is the length of the waist portion; that is, waist lines are following the same general tendencies as skirts, dropping to emphasize the long-line effects that Fashion favors more than ever this season.

Another difference, but this is noted in only a part of the styles, is the extreme simplicity of the models and their dependence on a novel use of self-trimming for their individuality. Such trimming, besides providing diversity in the mode, can be used in a variety of ways with charming results and generally with more assurance than embroidery, which must be artistically planned and skilfully executed for successfulness.

When such materials as crêpe de Chine with its elusive luster and chiffon in its transparent loveliness are chosen in so demure a color as pearl gray and combined in as simple a model as the blouse dress here pictured, self-trimming in petal effect seems to carry out, better than anything one can imagine, the very qualities suggested by the materials.

All the petals are of crêpe de Chine, the side panels and the sash being the only parts of the dress that are made of chiffon.

*Material and Pattern Requirements.*—About 4¼ yards of material 40 inches wide is required for the waist, the foundation skirt and the petals, and 1½ yards of the same width for the side panels and sash.

A plain-kimono blouse pattern, long-waisted in effect and having seam lines at each side back, is the only pattern you will need for cutting out the dress, unless you wish to gore the foundation skirt in order to take out some of the waist-line fulness. In this case, provide a slightly gored skirt pattern. If you have provided no skirt pattern, cut two straight sections for the skirt of the length you desire, plus allowance for the hem. In cutting the back waist section make allowance for a hem at the left side.

For the side panels, cut a piece several inches shorter than the desired skirt length and the full width of the material, and split this through the center lengthwise, thus forming a section for each side.

Cut strips straight across the fabric for the sash, making each of them about 7 inches wide. The combined length of the strips should be 2½ or 3 yards.

For the petal sections that finish the bottom of the side panels, cut four straight pieces, two about 6 inches wide and of a length that corresponds to the measurement of the lower edge of the panels and cut the other two about 10 inches wide. Cut similar pieces for the sleeves and sash ends.

*Construction.*—Join the sections provided for the skirt by means of pressed-open, overcasted seams. At the center back, make a short bound placket and then gather the waist line. Finish the waist opening by applying a narrow facing to the left back edge of the sleeved portion and hem the left edge of the back portion.

After stitching the seams of the waist, finish the right side-back seam by pressing the edges together back on the central portion and overcasting them. Finish the sleeve and under-arm seams by pressing them open and overcasting them, clipping the seam edges through the decidedly curved portion so as to prevent them from drawing. Then gather the waist line.

Make the side panels ready for application by having the long edges picoted or by finishing them with very narrow hems, and then gathering the waist line.

*Finishing the Petals.*—Mark the sections provided for finishing the lower edge of the panels and sleeves, and the ends of the sash, in order to divide the entire space into petals, leaving a seam allowance on both ends of the strips provided for the sleeves. You may find it necessary to make a slight difference in the width of the sleeve, sash, and skirt petals in order to utilize all the space and have no incomplete petals, but this difference will not be noticeable.

Also, mark the outline for the separate petals on any pieces of material you have left, shaping the petals as shown and making them about 4½ inches long.

Have all the outlines machine hemstitched, and then cut the hemstitching in two to form a picoted edge. Also, have the sash picoted at this time or bind it, if you prefer.

*Fitting.*—Put the waist portion on the figure and adjust and pin the fulness to a soft inside stay belt that has been made large enough to encircle the low waist line. Also, pin and adjust the skirt fulness to this, with the exception of the part between the waist and skirt closings, placing the pins at close intervals. Then turn the hem of the skirt.

Next, pin the side panels in place, and then pin the pieces provided for finishing the lower edge of these panels, letting the wider one extend 4 or 5 inches below the skirt hem, as illustrated, or so that merely the petals extend below the hem, if you prefer. Also, pin the petaled sections to the sleeves, making them any length you wish.

*Finishing.*—Stitch the waist, skirt, and panels to the belting and cover the raw edges on the right side with a narrow fold of self-material. Finish the skirt waist line separately from the waist opening to the center back.

Secure the petaled sections to the panels by laying them back over the panel, right sides together, and stitching along the straight edge of the petaled section; then let this petaled section fall down over the stitching so as to conceal it. Cut away the panel material that extends under the lower petaled section, turn under the edges, and whip them flat.

Tack the separate petals in position along the sides of the panels, securing merely the upper end of each and letting one overlap another.

Join the petaled sections to the sleeves in the manner you applied them to the skirt, but merely overcast the seam.

Finish the neck with a narrow facing.

---

## Fabrics Vary in Texture

Seldom has any one weave lent itself so successfully and with such popularity to cotton, silk, and woolen fibers as the éponge weave, which embraces homespun, ratiné, and many variations.

Other very prominent woolen fabrics are jersey and other knitted materials, the popular Kasha cloth, tweed, twills, such as serge and tricotine, and dressier fabrics of velvety texture.

In silks, the éponge weaves are not so numerous and consequently do not rank so high in favor as the crêpes. And when mention is made of crêpes, a multitude of exquisite variations come to mind. Some are in sheer weaves similar to Georgette crepe, and they range from this quality into very heavy weaves, many of them with a decided rib similar to faille. It is in the sports silks of this nature that very beautiful designs and colorings are noted. Printed silk, moiré, knitted silks, chiffon, and taffeta are all very promising for spring, also.

Besides the extremely popular éponge weaves in cotton, there are Japanese crêpes; gingham, which is particularly good in checks; printed cottons in endless array, including chintz, cretonne, sateen, and voile; tissue; organdie; and dotted Swiss. In addition to the figured voiles, plain, drop-stitch, and embroidered effects are in excellent standing.

Linens were never more colorful than they are this season. The favorite white naturally holds first place, but surely the appeal of the new colorings will be felt as the season advances.

Model 2

# Variations of Blouse Dress

**Model 2A.**—When a blouse boasts as new and as delightful a feature as a narrow yoke pointed on the shoulders and confining fulness at each side front and side back, the very best thing it can do is to emphasize this feature by abstaining from trimming and unessential seam lines. This type of yoke is particularly effective in a sheer material such as Georgette crêpe, the fabric selected in sand color for this model. The design is one that is suitable for the average or slender figure.

The skirt consists merely of a straight foundation with straight front and back panels. Bands of wool-embroidered filet net trim these panels and also the sleeves of the dress. The broad sash is of self-material. An enlarged detail of the embroidery is shown near the dress design. This is in the form of a darning-stitch run through the mesh of the net to form the desired outline.

For the average figure, provide 5 yards of material 40 inches wide and 3¼ yards of filet net banding 6 or 7 inches wide, with 8 small skeins of yarn. If you prefer, you may substitute fine lace for the filet banding.

To make a pattern for a yoke such as this, cut a plain kimono waist in muslin, and with this on the figure mark the outline of the yoke as you desire it. Cut on the marked lines and slash the waist portion of the muslin model at the side front and side back from the yoke line almost to the lower edge and separate the pieces to provide the desired fulness when placing the model on the material for cutting.

**Model 2B.**—Dent de lion, that delightful new yellow, shows unusual depth of color in rough-surfaced fabrics such as ratiné, of which this model is fashioned. Quite unusual is the manner in which the blouse portion is cut away at the center front to reveal a straight vest portion of very fine white voile. The voile collar, which is in narrow roll effect, fastens at the center front above the vest. The peasant sleeves, which are also of voile, have a lengthwise slash through the center, a feature that is very noticeable in spring and summer models.

So well liked were the side skirt panels of last season that Fashion did not hesitate to keep them on the spring calendar. These may be of the skirt length, but more often they are made from 2 to 5 inches longer than the skirt or, in extreme types of sheer dresses, as much as 10 inches longer.

The wool embroidery that adorns the straight belt, the drop shoulder effect, the cuff, and the vest outline is in harmonizing tones of orange, violet, and green, and the tassel that is suspended from the collar is of orange wool. An enlarged detail of the embroidery is shown at the upper left. This is in simple lazy-daisy design, with the exception of that outlining the vest, which is in darning-stitch.

This style made with narrow side panels requires, for the average figure, 3½ yards of material 36 inches wide, 1 yard of contrasting fabric, and 3 small skeins of yarn.

A casing is required at the waist-line joining of this model, so that elastic may be run through this and the dress permitted to be slipped on over the head. For a slender figure, the dress might be cut in one-piece fashion and supplied with a casing placed at a point you desire the waist line to be.

**Model 2C.**—Those who have found the bateau, or boat-shaped, neck line unbecoming or tiresome will welcome with enthusiasm the occasional square neck line that we are permitted to have this season. In many cases, as in this model, a very soft effect is produced by fulness gathered into a band. The drop shoulder, the knife-plaited side panels, the pin-tucked insertions, and the cuffs of white voile are all noteworthy features in this dress, which is made of orchid voile. Quite out of the ordinary is the straight belt of fine white linen embroidered in cross-stitch with soft tones of green, blue, and orange.

Provide about 5¾ yards of 40-inch material, with 1¼ yards of contrasting fabric and 2 small skeins of wool, for developing this design for the average figure.

You may have the tucked bands applied by means of machine hemstitching, or you may edge them with insertion of Val or in imitation of fagoting. If you have the time, you may prefer to secure them with hand fagoting, for this is one of the loveliest and most popular of spring trimmings.

**Model 2D.**—Nautical inspiration seems evident in this sports dress of white linen with its jaunty collar knotted at the waist opening in sailor fashion. On first thought, the skirt might not appear to have borrowed any detail from a mariner's costume, but the straps, after all, might be in imitation of naval stripes, even though they are in pairs and shifted from the usual position at the center side.

The embroidery in darning-stitch, as shown by the enlarged detail, is of bright-red mercerized floss. Over the joining of the skirt straps to the belt are placed cord rosettes, these consisting of coils of cord covered with self-material.

This type of dress is one that would be lovely if made of heavy sports silk in white or a bright color or in Canton crêpe in a dark or a light color.

Average requirements include 4½ yards of material 40 inches wide and 12 skeins of floss.

Finish the waist line of this dress as suggested for Model 2B.

**Model 2E.**—When both the material and the trimming of a dress are unusual, the gracious thing for a design to do is to make itself as unobtrusive as possible. A dress any simpler in cut than this style would be difficult to imagine, for it consists merely of a plain kimono bloused waist and a straight two-piece skirt rounded at each side in the manner illustrated. This style might prove hopelessly ordinary if it were not developed from a novel fabric, in this case red and white dimity, with trimming of a sharply contrasting nature, such as black Val lace, as shown. Even the girdle is quite out of the ordinary —tinsel and red ribbon with an attractive rosette closing.

Of material that is 36 inches wide, supply 3½ yards for developing this style for the average figure. Of the lace, 24 yards is needed, and of the ribbon, 5 yards.

**Model 2F.**—Undoubtedly sports influence, but so disguised that one hardly recognizes it, is responsible for the graceful scarf collar that contributes so much to the success of this costume of gray Georgette crêpe.

The dress is in practically two complete sections. The under section consists of a camisole lining of Georgette banded with wide cream-colored insertion and a straight gathered skirt having a band of insertion encircling the hip portion. The over-dress has a simple bloused waist with narrow, loose panels at the side front and side back, and wide front and back skirt portions left open at the sides, dropped to give the effect that is illustrated, and supplied with narrow panels that apparently are a continuation of those on the waist.

The manner in which most of the waist-line fulness of these skirt portions is concentrated at the sides in rows of shirring bespeaks Fashion's leaning to flat front and back effects.

The plaited, or braided, girdle, which is made of bands of satin in a soft tone of magenta, is finished at the side front with a flower made of this same fabric.

To make the dress, as illustrated, provide 6 yards of 40-inch material, 3¾ yards of insertion, and ½ yard of contrasting fabric for the girdle.

For the scarf collar, provide a straight piece of material about 7 inches wide and long enough to extend across the front and as far over each shoulder as you desire it.

2A

2B

2C

2E

2D

2F

# Three-Piece Costume

A season ago mention of a three-piece costume brought to mind a suit having a skirt portion extended or joined to contrasting material to form a dress. This year no such definite impression is created, for the three-piece costume goes masquerading in such unusual forms that one sometimes fails to recognize it as its true self.

Occasionally this costume really is in three pieces, having a separate blouse portion and a different color or material for each separate garment. Sometimes the regulation one-piece dress substitutes a cape of matching or contrasting fabric for the jacket. Other times the three-piece costume keeps its familiar form so far as parts are concerned, but assumes in the jacket a contrast in color that makes one think twice before classifying it. Again, the "knicker" suit comes in for its share of attention.

But the type that is most exasperating (that is, in so far as classification is concerned, but otherwise truly delightful) is the one that adopts a collared blouse and tops it with a sleeveless jacket having an armhole so tight and a neck line so simple that, to the uninitiated, the whole appears as a one-piece costume.

Of such a type, this model of navy serge is a variation, but here the illusion of the one-piece costume is even more effective, for the bands of serge secured in a cuff at the wrist line and held in the sleeveless armhole seem a distinct part of the bishop sleeve underneath.

The short box coat has a strip of fancy braid finishing the lower edge, a double band of the fabric finishing the front edges, and tie ends of ciré ribbon.

The skirt is of the straight knife-plaited variety.

The blouse of gray crêpe de Chine has its waist-line fulness confined in a wide belt of self-material. The high collar is a soft, crushed model. The blouse closing is effected by means of braid loops over self-covered buttons.

Sports or the heavy silks suitable for street wear, linen, and cottons, such as ratiné, are suitable for a costume· such as this, but if ratiné is used a gathered skirt should be substituted.

*Material and Pattern Requirements.*—This model requires, for the average figure, 3¼ yards of 54-inch fabric, 1⅛ yards of fancy braid, 1 yard of ribbon, and 2 yards of contrasting material for the waist.

For the skirt, cut off a length of the material equal to twice the skirt length you desire, plus twice the width you wish to make the hems. From this length cut a strip along one selvage 10 to 15 inches wide, depending on the width you wish your skirt. Then cut the remaining piece in half for the two lengths.

For the sleeveless jacket, provide a box-coat pattern that fits snugly through the shoulders and has a natural armhole.

Cut the jacket long enough to extend under the trimming braid at the lower edge. From the piece taken from the skirt lengths, cut straight strips about 4 inches wide and of the required length to finish the front edges, and strips about 5 inches wide and long enough to extend over the puff, as illustrated, for straps to complete the sleeves.

For cutting the blouse, use a long-waisted bloused pattern having a high collar, or one in Peter Pan effect, if you prefer, and a full bishop sleeve having a close armhole line.

For the waist-line band, cut a straight strip about 9 inches wide and 3 inches longer than the low waist-line measurement.

*Making the Skirt.*—Before plaiting the skirt, stitch both seams, press these seams open, and secure the hem in the lower edge. Then, starting at the center of one of the pieces, lay the plaits into a measurement equal to half a loosely taken hip measurement, and afterwards treat the other side in a similar manner, turning the plaits on each side toward the center back.

For the placket, slash the left side front at the inside edge of one of the plaits and bind these edges.

Then pin the plaited section to an inside stay belting, making, from the waist line, any adjustment in length that may be necessary. Next, stitch the plaits to the belting and cover the raw edges with silk seam binding.

*Making the Blouse.*—Join the shoulder, under-arm, and sleeve edges as French seams. Stitch the sleeves in position in a plain seam, trim the seam allowance to a scant ¼ inch, and bind the raw edges together with a bias strip of material.

A facing cut 1 inch wide is required for the right front of the blouse. Before applying this, baste the braid loops in position so that when the facing strip is turned back to the wrong side the loops will extend out from the turned edge and the ends will be concealed by the facing strip.

Face the collar edges and also the joining of the collar to the blouse. Then secure stays in each side of the collar.

Finish a short opening in the lower end of the sleeve seam with a narrow bias binding; then gather the lower edge of the sleeve and confine it in a close-fitting wrist binding, a trifle less than 1 inch wide when finished.

Apply the waist-line band as a binding, also, thus securing the waist-line fulness and providing a neat finish.

*Making the Jacket.*—After basting the shoulder and under-arm seams, try on the jacket and make any adjustment necessary to produce a snug fit through the shoulders.

Then stitch the shoulder and under-arm seams, press them open, and bind the edges with bias silk or seam binding.

Make the sleeve straps as you would a narrow belt, but press them so that the seam line is at the center.

Turn the correct line at the lower edge of the coat when it is on the figure, turning the seam allowance to the right side. Also, pin the straps in position at the armhole and into a straight wrist band cut 2¾ or 3 inches wide and just a trifle larger than the wrist band of the blouse.

Finish the armholes with bias facings of silk and secure the straps at the wrist in the strip provided for the binding.

Slip-stitch the braid to the lower edge of the jacket, apply the bands to the front edges as wide bindings, and then face the neck edge.

---

## Footwear Shows Sports Influence

It must be a lazy or indifferent foot nowadays that does not keep pace with its wearer's fancy in frocks and wraps, for surely there is sufficient diversity in footwear styles to satisfy even the most exacting and most sensitive supporter of femininity. With sports apparel taking the lead in garments, the sports influence is naturally reflected in footwear. Many of the sports shoes are startling or extreme in design, but their "roomy" last and low, broad heels supply the very essence of comfort. Two-color combinations are noted in the most novel of sports oxfords, black and white, tan and brown, tan and white predominating and both strap and lace styles being favored.

In the "dress-up" models, patent-leather leads, sometimes alone, but with especial smartness when it is combined with gray suède. Gray is a dominant note in the dressy types, suède and fine kid each being shown.

Straps are still considered the smartest detail in design, with buckles rather than buttons the desired fastening; but the simple low pump remains in favor, while a higher built pump with elastic inserts at the sides and a pump of colonial style are vying for popular favor. Leniency in regard to the height of the heel is notable, even in dressy models.

Model 3

# Variations of Three-Piece Costume

*Model 3A.*—Crêpe-knit, that delightfully soft and lustrous silk which has a surface very similar to fine Turkish toweling but is backed by a jersey weave, was chosen in pumpkin color for the cape and principal dress fabric of this costume.

It would have been a very easy matter to let the one material form the entire model, but nowadays, when practically all other three-piece costumes boast a two- or three-material combination, even so lovely a fabric as crêpe-knit feels in duty bound to ally with another material.

White crêpe de Chine was the selection. It is used generously for the sleeves, which are in peasant, or bishop, style, but otherwise forms only the narrow fitted yoke of the one-piece dress. Due prominence, however, is given to the sleeves, for the cape is provided with deep, graceful armhole lines.

The costume developed as illustrated for the average figure requires 5 yards of material 40 inches wide, with ¾ yard of contrasting fabric.

In cutting out the dress, use a one-piece, kimono-sleeve pattern having shoulder and hip-line seams. Mark on this a yoke of the depth you desire; then trace the yoke pattern if you wish the dress cut to extend up under the yoke.

Use a bishop-sleeve pattern for cutting out the sleeves and in the development of a muslin model, and set these into the dropped armhole line so that they hang properly, afterwards cutting away the surplus material above the joining line.

In making a muslin model for the cape collar, use a straight strip of material, gather it in at the back neck line, and draw it under the cape edge a trifle at the front to make the Tuxedo revers-like portions narrower than the back collar.

In making the cape, use a wide facing for the armhole edges.

*Model 3B.*—As if the brightness of verdigris green, the color of the Roshanara crepe that forms the skirt and cape of this costume, were not enough to satisfy a color-hungry public, the blouse of white crêpe de Chine has chosen for its decoration all-over embroidery designs in black combined with parrot colorings that harmonize and make a very pleasing contrast with the fabric color.

Another note of black is found in the wooden beads that decorate the trimming band at the center front of the blouse. This note is repeated again on the edges of the cape, which, although extreme in its simplicity of cut, consisting of merely a straight piece of material, appears quite out of the ordinary.

The skirt, as well as the cape, boasts a scarf finished with wooden-bead fringe trimming in colors that match the embroidery of the blouse. This is placed at the left side and extended into the waist portion, thus establishing a closer relationship between the skirt and the blouse.

Material requirements for the average figure include 3½ yards 36 or 40 inches wide, 1¼ yards of contrasting fabric, and 6 skeins of embroidery floss.

If you wish, you may substitute figured silk for the waist portion, or you may use cotton ratiné for the skirt and cape and printed cotton or plain linen for the blouse.

In cutting out the material, provide for the cape a straight piece of material 27 inches wide and 1 yard long, and for the scarf, a straight strip 11 inches wide and 1¼ yards long.

In making the cape, let the longer sides form the upper and lower edges and join the cape and scarf portions for 10 or 11 inches across the back neck line.

Cut the blouse portion with the aid of a long-waisted kimono blouse pattern and the skirt with a comparatively straight pattern having fulness at the back waist line.

*Model 3C.*—That even the browns and tans of this season have a gustatory as well as an esthetic appeal is evidenced by the names the brown and tan of this model inspired, fudge and

taffy, respectively. The unobtrusiveness of this color combination and of the material, Canton crêpe, only serves to emphasize the striking novelty of the design.

A seam line simulating a sleeve is noted at the front of the cape, and the center-back portion is bloused at a low waist line, these two details providing the effect of a wrap. The embroidery is of heavy silk floss developed in motifs of a design shown enlarged at the left of the model.

At the left of the back view of the cape is shown the front view of the dress that forms a part of the costume. This is a blouse model having a wide front skirt panel dropped at the sides to make pointed extensions below the skirt hem, and a waist portion that relies almost entirely on its very unusual sleeve for novelty of design.

Provide, for the average figure, 5¼ yards of 40-inch fabric, 1¼ yards of contrasting color, and 1 small bunch of chenille floss.

For the cape, you will need a special pattern. This may be developed in muslin cut with the aid of a plain cape pattern.

*Model 3D.*—When navy Poiret twill is used in a three-piece costume, its favorite combination seems to be with hues of red, sometimes in a woolen fabric but more often in the silks of crêpe weave. In this instance, vermilion crêpe de Chine used for the overblouse of the costume forms a striking contrast, but as so much of the blouse is covered by the cape, the general effect is not startling nor extreme.

Dull gold-thread embroidery, applied in darning-stitches that follow a design shown in detail at the bottom of the page, decorates the front lower edge of the blouse and the joining of the sleeve material to the wide band of Poiret twill. As the blouse is a slip-over model, it is provided with a slash from the neck line at the center front and a casing at the back waist line, through which an elastic is drawn and over which sash ends brought from the under arms are tied.

A circular cut and a yoke extended to form scarf ends characterize the cape of the costume, while the skirt is a straight, simple one that may be attached to an inside stay belting or made with a loose waist line and applied to a camisole lining.

For the average figure, 2½ yards of 54-inch fabric, 1⅝ yards of 40-inch material, and 3 skeins of floss are needed, with 2 yards of ciré ribbon for the tie ends at the neck line.

*Model 3E.*—Knicker suits might have materialized to an even greater extent in the fall if, in many instances, they had not been adopted by extremists for purposes other than those for which they were introduced. This season, however, the knicker suit, for outdoor activities and sports wear, has become an accomplished fact, for the true out-of-doors or sports lover has found this costume so practical, comfortable, and modest that she is not at all adverse to accepting it for its special purpose.

A decided innovation in knicker costumes, this cotton khaki suit has, for town wear, a skirt made of two straight pieces of material gathered at the waist line and joined to separate belt portions, the front piece being supplied with buttonholes along both lengthwise edges and the back piece having buttons to correspond. The facing applied on the right side to the lower edge may be omitted if desired.

Whenever the skirt would prove a hindrance, it may be unbuttoned and raised to the shoulder, then merely the belts buttoned together to form a "fence" collar, the fulness of the front section confined by the belt of the knickerbockers, and the skirt back permitted to fall free, thus transforming the costume into a modish cape affair of singular distinction.

About 4¾ yards of 36-inch material or 2¼ yards of 44-inch fabric is enough for the skirt and knickerbockers. The simple blouse may be made of natural-colored pongee, white linen, or a serviceable cotton, 2 yards of 36-inch material being required.

3 a

3 B

3 c

3 D

3 e

# Draped Dress

To an artist, the word draped in dressmaking usually means beauty of line; to the beginner in sewing, a real puzzle to solve. But this season's drape is different, for in most cases it means only a little pinch or fulness in the placing of the fabric to develop the drape. And when the drape in the skirt is simply an extension on the front, it makes no problem at all.

At first thought, one selects the heavy silks for drapery, the soft, heavy Canton crêpes, for instance. The heavier crêpes are in high favor for the smartest dresses, and embroidery is daintier and more exquisite than in many previous seasons.

In this case, the dress is of reseda green Canton crêpe with gold embroidery. The back of the blouse is the same as the front, the preference being given to the front, in that the girdle, with its attractive roses of self-material and wee gold centers, terminates there.

The dent de lion yellow with pale green or white embroidery is smart for color. Then, of course, there are the periwinkle blue and the grays that Fashion heralds just now, and the navy that some always delight in. All these colors are exceptionally good for such a dress, especially when the material is heavy enough in texture to give grace to the lines.

Chiffon of harmonizing color is used for facing the skirt draperies, but these may be merely picoted, if preferred.

*Material and Pattern Requirements.*—The blouse effect of the waist requires, of course, a foundation lining, 1¼ yards of 36-inch material being sufficient for this, and 4½ to 5 yards of 40-inch material is needed for the dress. For the embroidery, supply from 4 to 6 small skeins of floss, according to the design.

For cutting out the blouse portion of the dress, supply a pattern having loose lines, a bateau neck line, and a side-front waist closing. Or, if you prefer, you may use simply a plain foundation-waist pattern.

No pattern is needed for the development of the skirt.

*Cutting.*—If you are using a plain foundation-waist pattern, to acquire the loose effect in the blouse, slash the front and back portions of the pattern lengthwise through the center from the lower edge almost to the shoulder line. Then separate the slashed edges 1 to 2½ inches at the lower edge, this depending on the amount of fulness desired.

Mark on the pattern the bateau neck line, the side-front closing, and the side-back seam line. Then, in using the pattern, cut the right front of the blouse to extend a seam's width beyond the left side closing, and cut the left front only wide enough to extend from the under arm a seam's width beyond the side closing. Follow practically this same method in cutting the back, but arrange for the seam at the right rather than at the left side.

The upper part of the sleeve can be cut from the top of a one-piece sleeve that fits the armhole of the foundation pattern used. For the lower portion of the sleeve, cut a straight strip of muslin as wide as the measurement of the lower edge of the sleeve and about ¾ yard long. Fold this crosswise through the center and pin the ends together to the sleeve so that the long open edges are on top of the arm. Make this of an individually becoming length.

The skirt is made of two widths of material, each piece tacked under the other and 10 inches of the material allowed to extend out to form the drapery. This drapery is faced back with self-material a good 14 inches in order to conceal the edge well and to give additional weight to the dress.

The subtle little straight panel 12 to 14 inches wide at the right side relieves the plainness over the hip and gives an opportunity for embroidery, which intensifies interest in the dress.

The abandon in line is the effect to work for in developing such a dress. To insure good results, it is well first to cut and fit perfectly a muslin model; then, when the dress is cut from this, it can be made almost entirely before it is assembled.

*Making.*—When the dress itself is cut out, join the shoulders, press the seams open, mark for all the embroidery, and apply all of the designs at this time. Then prepare to face the neck edge and the embroidered side edges of the front and back.

The neck edges should be finished with a fitted facing 1½ inches wide and the side edges, with a straight facing 2½ inches wide. The corners where the facings meet should be carefully mitered so as to avoid bulk. The free edge should be tacked in two or three places but not securely fastened, as this would give a set appearance.

Have both long edges of the sleeve extensions finished with picoting. Then, after doubling each strip crosswise through the center, pin it to the lower edge of the sleeve as you did in the muslin model. Next, stitch it in position, and after cutting away the surplus under-seam allowances, turn under the upper allowance and whip it to the sleeve, taking great care not to make the stitches evident on the right side.

Next, face back the skirt pieces, joining them by placing the right sides together and stitching across the top, down the side, and across the bottom.

As the lower edge of the skirt is cut straight and the drapery itself gives the irregular finish, the hem can be put in before the waist-line joining is made.

Gather the upper edge of the skirt from the termination of the faced portion around the remainder of the waist line.

Face the panel for the right side and place this so that the back edge extends underneath the back drapery. Secure this with the stitches you take to join the back edge of the front skirt portion underneath the side-back drapery.

Form the under-arm seam, sew in the sleeves, and proceed to put the dress together. This should be done on the figure or on a dress form, so that the location of the drape, the portion of the left side panel, and the blouse of the waist will be in right position to be entirely becoming. In accomplishing this, you will find that a close study of the illustration will help in keeping the style effect, which is second only to becomingness.

The waist line, which is concealed by an 11-inch bias girdle of self-material, is easy and comes just to the top of the hips. No stitching should be visible on the dress to interfere with the beauty of the embroidery, and all the finishing and tacking stitches should be taken with great care in order not to detract from the gracefulness of the design.

It is interesting to observe that the wide girdle of a year ago is definitely smart this season. Its popularity may be due to its favoring the corsetless figure and giving body to the waist line in the absence of the corset. Suppleness and grace, however, are the effect to work for, at present, whether a corset is worn or not.

---

## Sheer Hosiery Is the Vogue

For wear with sports shoes, wool stockings in tweed colorings and black and white are used in greatest abundance, although new lisle and silk styles are also employed. But sheer silk is the rule for the ultra dressy models and is considered especially chic when it is of beige, almond, nude, putty color, or gray and worn with a dark or a partially dark pump.

Clocks in openwork effect or embroidered in white or high colors on dark grounds, or vice versa, drop-stitch, and all-over lace effects in rather large designs are suggested as an occasional change from the plain stocking.

*Model 4*

# Variations of Draped Dress

*Model 4A.*—A smart dress should be self-evident and the tricks of achievement should be so subtly concealed that the effect and not the details is noticeable. In this delightfully sheer frock of periwinkle-blue Georgette and gold-colored lace, simplicity and daintiness are at once evident. The lace is not of the metallic kind, but is of a fine, delicate nature that makes it especially suitable for combination with sheer crêpe.

There is a foundation, held straight and close, of sheer flesh-colored chiffon under the blouse portion to permit the blouse to fall down easily and gracefully from the neck without evidence of sewing. For this, a band of gold cloth might be substituted, if desired. This would add considerable richness to the general effect, and would be especially lovely for evening wear. For a summer daytime dress, however, the chiffon seems more suitable.

The foundation waist opens at the left side in the back and continues down with the placket. The overblouse hooks on the left shoulder, and the side drapery is so arranged that the opening of the dress is not visible.

For development, 5¼ yards of Georgette, ½ yard of chiffon, and 3¼ yards of lace are needed.

The foundation skirt is of 1¾ widths of the 40-inch Georgette. A band of the lace is set in by means of picoting or a rolled hem at a becoming point across the hips. The two drapery pieces, which in this case are 40 inches wide and of the skirt length, are put over the foundation, veiling the lace except at the sides. Of course, picot edges or rolled hems are necessary for all the edges that require finishing and either finish is attractive for such a dress.

The sleeve portions are of the lace, shaped in on the shoulder by means of a semi-bias picoted seam. The lace is then sewed to the armhole in as inconspicuous a way as possible.

A narrow ribbon girdle is used around the waist, and to this wee roses are attached two-thirds of the way across the front, the ribbon extending around and tying in a bow at the center back.

*Model 4B.*—The chemise draped dress is, for slender or stout, a real favorite, for it can be made to fit loose and conceal slenderness, or it can be made to hug close and not be bulky.

Drapery, as shown in this dress, is a new, artistic touch for spring that sets out to be much favored, because young or old, stout or slender, can use such drapery in a becoming way.

Embroidered crêpe de Chine of medium light blue is used for the dress, with sleeves and side-gore drapes of soft black taffeta. These side pieces of taffeta are gores set in and allowed to come down in points at the side, thus giving an irregular hem line. The joining of the contrasting material in the skirt is made soft and pleasing by a fold or plait of the crêpe laid over the seam line so that the seam falls at the inside edge of this plait.

The roses of taffeta at the sides are attractive and give to the drapery a terminating point that adds much to the attractiveness of the dress.

The chiffon sleeve bands in hoop effect can be omitted and a longer sleeve provided if a more practical style is required.

If desired, a narrow, straight-around sash may be used instead of the unbroken waist line.

This dress is interesting when developed in blue cloth or soft, heavy satin, and it has excellent possibilities in the sheerer materials, if a one-piece slip is provided underneath for a suitable foundation.

To make a dress of this design for the average figure, provide 3 yards of material 36 or 40 inches wide, 1½ yards of contrasting fabric of the same width, and 1 yard of sheer material, provided sleeves of the kind illustrated are desired.

*Model 4C.*—This model has its inspiration in its sleeve and skirt. It has been a long time since Fashion dared to show a leg-o'-mutton sleeve so boldly, though one can see at once that 'tis the sleeve that gives the ultra smart effect to the slip-on blouse with which we are all familiar.

In comparison with the type of sleeve that was formerly regarded as the leg-o'-mutton, the modern interpretation seems to carry off the honors. One of the principal reasons may be because of the fabrics that are now usually employed for these sleeves—sheer, fascinating weaves that carry the fulness in such an engaging manner. But, again, it may be for the reason that the extra size now drops from the armhole, instead of being held in stiff, gathered folds to form a puff that stood considerably higher than the shoulder line.

It takes but a comparison of the two to bring the realization that the 1922 leg-o'-mutton is by far a more youthful and more graceful style than the original stiff, lined, and puffed sleeve.

The way in which this dress of Canton and printed crêpe is arranged to get into is interesting, for, as you know, the only opening is at the center front across the waist line. The back is cut in one piece as for a chemise dress. The whole dress slips over the head; then the snugness at the waist line is achieved by the front drape drawn across and secured in place.

The spider-web shirring is extremely smart and new; that is, we consider it new because it has not been fashionable for such a long time. This shirring is much in evidence on the beautiful printed black crêpes, which are so interesting in design as to make one forget that their color is black.

Average material requirements include 4½ yards of crêpe and 1¼ yards of contrasting sheer material.

*Model 4D.*—The extreme in the season's drape is in evidence here. A dress of this type is the French modiste's delight, for she can pull and pucker the lovely fabric to get just the smart ensemble that she seems to live to achieve.

For a dinner or semi-evening dress, this is a very pleasing type, and its style value is so high that one could wear it for some time with delight and assurance. A simpler type of blouse as a variation is shown at the right of the front view of the dress.

To make the dress, there will be required 4½ yards of lovely soft satin, 1¼ yards of exquisitely dainty lace, a handsome ornament for the girdle, and a goodly bit of determination to accomplish the style effect evidenced.

'Tis not that the dress is difficult to do; but it needs just the right start, and this should be a semifitted princesse slip of soft silk that extends to the knees and has an inside stay belt to hold it at the waist line.

Put the slip on the dress form and place the blouse portion over this; then begin the very interesting part—the draping of the skirt.

First, take a full width of the material that measures on the length the hip measure, plus 8 to 10 inches, for freedom, as the skirt is made with the lengthwise thread going around. Place a pin half way on the selvage of one side, pin this point to the side seam high up on the right side of the slip, bring the material around the form and together at the left side, laying it in folds down the seam every 6 or 8 inches to get the draped effect. Pin this edge together so that it can be sewed later.

To arrange the double-cascade drape that hangs over the seam, cut two pieces of material in triangular form, the upper edge measuring about 12 inches and the material tapering to nothing at the points. The cascades should be made of two thicknesses of material or faced with chiffon in order to have sufficient weight.

After the drape is developed, the soft bias girdle is easily draped around the figure and fastened underneath the ornament.

4 a

4 B

4 C

4 D

# Basque Dress

What more can one ask of Fashion than that she retain the basque dress in its entrancingly youthful interpretation and add a few distinctly new touches to set it definitely apart from its predecessors? Surely, one would not consider that it be laid aside as long as its development contains any such delightful possibilities as this model of yellow crêpe knit.

The unique closing is effected by the surplice bodice studded in double-breasted fashion with large crystal buttons.

Starting out in a very conservative manner, the sleeve abruptly extends into an exaggerated cuff, and from this drops a wide frill of white mousseline completely covered with narrow ruffles.

The proportions of the collar are quite in keeping with those of the under sleeves, but this, rather than being completely covered with ruffles, has merely a wide banding of them.

Two full widths of material form the skirt, thus providing considerable fulness at the waist line.

This model is one that lends itself to any of the bright colors in crêpe-knit, as well as to brown, blue, and black for spring street wear. Also, it might be made of the heavier crêpe-silk weaves or of cotton homespun or crêpe for midsummer wear.

In place of the mousseline collar and under sleeves, organdie might be used with ruffles of self-material or of fine net.

*Material and Pattern Requirements.*—Of material that is 36 inches wide, 4 yards is required for this model, with 1¼ yards of one kind of material for the collar and under sleeves, or 1 yard for the foundation pieces and ½ yard for the ruffles, provided they are to be made of different materials.

For cutting out the basque, provide a semifitting, surplice-front pattern with side-back seam lines.

Develop a muslin model for the sleeve, shaping the arm-hole and seam lines as far as the elbow with the aid of a two-piece pattern, providing enough width in the upper section for the fulness that is held by rows of shirring, as shown, and leaving ample material below the ends of the back seam line to provide a cuff effect of the size you desire. Then, when the muslin model is on the arm, shape the extensions as you wish them, piecing the muslin model if extra material is needed to produce the effect you want. A sleeve formed in this manner will have an open space between the cuff effect and the shirred edge of the sleeve proper.

You may form the collar pattern, also, by modeling it in muslin, placing a lengthwise thread at the center back, and laying the muslin in deep folds if you intend to use a soft material for trimming, or using a wide true-bias strip, if the collar is to be of organdie.

In shaping the muslin model for the under sleeve, you may find the use of a broad, flared sleeve pattern helpful.

For the skirt, cut two full widths of material, each equal to the skirt length you desire, plus allowance for a hem.

*Making.*—Join the two pieces provided for the skirt, using plain, pressed-open seams, and clip the selvages at intervals of several inches so that they will not draw. Leave the upper end of the left seam open for about 8 inches and finish this opening as a flat-stitched continuous placket. Then gather the upper edge.

The most satisfactory way of finishing this dress is to attach the skirt to a waist lining. Make this in the usual manner, with an opening at the center front, but do not gather the waist line nor attach it to an inside belting.

Baste the basque waist and sleeve seams for the fitting.

*Fitting.*—With the lining on the figure, lay the waist-line fulness into darts at each side front and side back, fitting to give a moderately loose effect. Then mark a waist line from ¼ to ½ inch higher than you desire the waist line of the basque and turn under the lining on this line. Pin this over the skirt, adjusting the fulness carefully and leaving the lining and skirt separate from the center front to the left under-arm seam. Then turn the hem in the lower edge of the skirt.

Try the basque on over the waist lining, and observe the various points that should be noted in the fitting.

*Finishing.*—Stitch the waist lining to the skirt and, after trimming away the surplus material underneath, face the raw edges of the joining. Bind the waist line of the skirt from the center front to the left under-arm seam.

Stitch the basque in plain seams and press them open. If any of the seams are decidedly curved, clip the allowance to make them lie flat. Then either face or hem the vertical edges of the surplice portions and the lower edge of the basque.

Make the sleeves ready by first applying rows of shirring to the upper sleeve sections and facing this edge. Then finish the sleeves in French or plain overcasted seams. Join the cuff edges with plain seams, and then face the entire extended portions, extending these facings around the entire lower edge. Insert the sleeves with plain seams, and press the seam edges together back on the basque portion and bind or overcast them.

Make the ruffles ready by having them picoted on both edges so that they will be about 1 inch wide when finished and then gathering them along one picoted edge. Apply one ruffle to the very edge of the collar and cuffs and baste the others in position. Then secure them by machine or by hand.

Join the collar to the basque with a plain seam. Then trim the allowance on the basque to within ⅛ or ¼ inch, turn the edge of the collar allowance over this, and whip the turned edge flat to the basque. Join the under sleeves at least 1 inch above the lower edge of the cuff by whipping the turned edge to the cuff facing.

To complete the dress, tack the basque to the lining at the shoulder and under arm and across the back waist line, leaving the surplice fronts to close separately.

---

## Garden-Flower Colors Rule

After several seasons in which black has been the dominant note, even rather subdued colors would appear bright and cheery, but with the new colors showing such a decided reaction against black, they seem to have a startling brilliance in comparison.

The colors that have been promised for spring and summer other than white, which is unquestionably recommended for mid-summer wear, may be likened unto those of an old-fashioned garden in which, from early spring until late summer, appear an amazing array of colors.

Yellow copied from the dandelion is having a decided vogue at present. This, through the various hues of orange, with emphasis on tangerine, leads to scarlet and pure red, upon which much emphasis is placed, and on to the bluish reds.

Blues vary from the light, pure tones to navy, through the violet-tinged hue in which periwinkle is most often mentioned, and in several hues touched by green or gray.

Greens, in many instances, flaunt their pure brilliance, but again appear in grayed moss and sage varieties.

For spring and summer wear, browns are in excellent favor. These range from delicate tans to the deep wood and tobacco tones, beige being a color that is decidedly in the foreground.

Grays in pure and colored varieties are also very popular.

In spite of the appeal of the brilliant colors, not all attention has been diverted from black, for it is still used for a great many suits and street dresses, but usually it is enlivened by a touch of color that dispels any suggestion of somberness. And when combined with white, the white usually being greatly in the ascendency, the result is one that this season stamps as truly smart.

Model 5

*Look for a collectible print version at the end of this issue.*

# Variations of Basque Dress

*Model 5A.*—The simplicity and youthfulness of this dress with its basque and front-yoke effect take it right into favor with many, especially those who desire smartness and yet insist upon serviceability.

And as for materials, any of the season's smart fabrics that possess enough body to pinch up nicely in the little drapes at the sides of the blouse and can hang with ease and surety in a half-circular skirt may be selected. The buttons on the skirt are of self-material. Ornamental buttons or a simple tailor-stitched line may be substituted, if desired.

The sleeves and the skirt are secured to a semifitted foundation lining and the basque blouse portion opens half way on the left shoulder and 6 or 8 inches up from the bottom of the left side seam. This allows enough opening to permit the blouse to go over the head comfortably.

The under sleeves of Georgette are quite full, measuring nearly 20 inches at the lower edge and 15 inches at the top. They are gathered top and bottom and joined to the upper sleeve in a plain seam, and the lower edge is simply arranged in a tiny wristband in peasant effect. A bias fold of Georgette hugs the neck quite innocently, yet serves to relieve the plainness.

Provide for the average figure 4½ yards of 36-inch material and ½ yard of sheer fabric.

*Model 5B.*—The aristocracy that taffeta evidences is enough to make all other fabrics envious, especially when it has the distinction of being made up in so smart a style. Soft, shining black taffeta makes the dress, while mist-color chiffon is used for the plaited portions and tiny black velvet bows serve as ornaments. Bias facings neatly stitched on the side ornament the edges of the little basque and finish them as well.

The sleeves, with their wee opening at the tip of the shoulder, the vest, closing at the top and the bottom, the basque with its lower edge in points, and the straight-around and zigzag pin tucks of the skirt, all boast of springtime newness.

The pointed skirt is a compromise for the longer skirt, and is attractive when the skirt boasts of just the right fulness.

Georgette may be used as a more serviceable substitute for chiffon. And for a truly summer frock, organdie substitutes admirably for taffeta, while sheer net serves equally well for the chiffon.

For the average figure, 4 yards of 36-inch material and ½ yard of contrasting fabric are needed.

*Model 5C.*—One needs youth and a slight figure to know all the delights of organdie, but when dotted Swiss makes the frock itself, then these characteristics cease to be entirely essential.

Gray Swiss with pink dots and pink organdie make a smart combination, or white Swiss with yellow or red dots and white organdie are beautiful in this basque model.

The blouse with its tiny sleeves and apron sash, which tucks under the front panel portion of the blouse, adds novelty to the dress design. A piece of bias material is shaped to fit the armhole and at the same time cup over the armhole in a way to give a right foundation for the little sleeve ruffles.

The ladder work made from bias strips of organdie is new and pleasing and combines well with the ruffles, though these may be omitted if one finds it necessary to subdue the fulness over the hips. Cross-stitches ½ inch deep or even darning-stitches serve as a good substitute for the ruffles on the organdie, the purpose being to relieve the plainness of the side panels.

This model requires, for the average figure, 4¼ yards of dotted Swiss and 2½ yards of organdie.

*Model 5D.*—Sleeveless dresses are always a delight because they must be worn by those who have pretty arms and who use them gracefully. And since the style of this sleeveless model is so very pretty and smart as well, one can defiantly add sleeves and still have a very beautiful frock. The omission of sleeves makes possible a delightfully smart evening gown.

This original model was especially beautiful made of tea-rose pink crêpe de Chine and decorated with alluring opalescent bugle beads. It would be pretty, also, in voile or Georgette. Of any of the materials, 5½ yards would be required.

The blouse is made over a foundation lining to which under-arm sections of material are placed, these extending up and around the armhole for 2 inches, so as to conceal the lining. The front and the back of the blouse are really straight panels shaped a bit at the neck and secured in place on the shoulders and at the waist line.

Straight strips of material form the sleeve extensions. These are attached only the depth of the armhole.

The skirt consists of a foundation underskirt, which may have a sham top above the knees. The panels are interesting because they are so simple. Still, they need to be proportioned correctly for the individual and placed with like consideration.

*Model 5E.*—The nice black dress of our grandmothers' time was of moiré. That dress makes the picture for many when moiré is mentioned, while others, of course, immediately think of moiré as a hat or dress trimming.

This year, moiré has marched right out and taken a preferred front seat with the most fastidious fabrics. And the younger you are, the more you will delight in the moiré of today, for it possesses the body of taffeta yet the grace of the loveliest crêpes. Its luster spells newness and at the same time assures one of much serviceability.

Lace, net, chiffon, Georgette, batiste, or organdie is smart with moiré, so you may have your choice of material for the ruffles, which should be made up exquisitely dainty to provide a right setting for the moiré.

For this model, a foundation lining in brassière effect with straps over the shoulder is admirable, because the ruffles can be attached to it and thus held comfortably in place.

Two straight widths of material are used in the skirt. The seams are covered with a bias strip 1½ inches wide when finished, and over this is carefully slip-stitched another bias strip measuring ½ inch wide when finished. These tend to give length to the skirt, cover the seams, and at the same time lend interest to the dress.

Material requirements include 4¼ yards 36 inches wide and ½ yard for the ruffles.

*Model 5F.*—This model seems to want to be christened the Handkerchief Sash Dress, yet because of its blouse coming over the skirt in rather snug fashion, it has to be reckoned with as one of the basque variety.

The material of the dress is of English print in a grayed orange and white trimmed with fine sateen in a matching tone of grayed orange, 4½ yards of the print and 1 yard of sateen being required for the average figure.

The underneath skirt is plain, being made of 1¾ widths of material. The placket opening is made on a seam and arranged to come under the left side front, so as to be concealed.

The skirt is secured to the foundation lining, which has its opening at the left side front, and thus permits the vest to be placed in position on the lining. Also, the opening of the waist meets that in the skirt.

All the pattern edges are carefully marked, the foundation lines sewed together, and the seams marked for picoting. Then, all edges are picoted, even the bottom of the skirt. Rolled hems serve excellently if time is available and machine hemstitching is not. And, again, the edges may be bound if the material is firm enough to permit of its being done well.

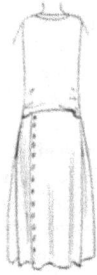

5 A

5 B

5 C

5 D

5 E

5 F

# Raglan-Tuxedo Suit

How strange it is that no book of synonyms classifies spring-time and suit-time together. One needs but to venture out on the first springlike day to wonder why one ever imagined that any smartness could be evidenced by a voluminous coat with a fur collar of smothering dimensions. And following this thought comes the realization that a tailored suit worn with an immaculate blouse is the very height of sartorial perfection and consequently of comfort. Is there any wonder that springtime and suit-time cannot well afford to be separated?

Spring suits almost invariably favor youthful designs, for youthfulness fits in so well with the spirit of the season. This year shows no exception to the general rule, for short box coats are in the majority, kimono and raglan sleeves have a place in suit styles, and skirts maintain their straight, unfitted lines and are shorter in length than dresses of most types.

These youthful features, together with a soft Tuxedo collar, a jaunty tie of grosgrain ribbon, roomy patch pockets, flaring sleeves, and a skirt made less severe by overlying folds, or panels, make this model of blue Kasha cloth. The buttons are of composition in a blue that matches the fabric.

Many suits of this type are being developed from silk this season. Of the silks, those of heavy crêpe or novelty sports weave may be used to best advantage.

*Material and Pattern Requirements.*—Of material that is 54 inches wide, 4 yards is required, with 2 yards of ribbon and 8 buttons. If you wish a lining, provide 2 yards of silk.

For cutting out the jacket, you will need a box-coat pattern having raglan sleeves. If the sleeves do not have considerable width, flare the seam line when cutting out the muslin model. In case the pattern is not open at the front, as illustrated, turn back the fronts when the muslin model is on the figure. Then form the Tuxedo-collar pattern by modeling it in muslin, letting a straight grain extend down the fronts and curving the material around toward the center back, where a bias seam will be necessary. Exercise the greatest care in developing the muslin model, for it is essential that it be fitted and that each seam line be becomingly placed before the suit fabric is cut.

For cutting the skirt, provide a comparatively straight pattern having some fulness at the waist line.

*Cutting.*—Be particularly careful about placing the pattern pieces on the material, seeing that a lengthwise thread extends through the center of each section.

For each of the pockets, cut a straight piece of material about 6 inches wide and 7 inches long and round off the lower corners. Using this piece as a guide, cut shorter pieces to face the portion of the pocket that extends below the jacket.

For the skirt panels, cut strips several inches longer than the skirt length and 5½ or 6 inches wide, and for the belt, a strip several inches longer than the waist measurement and 3 inches wide.

If you have provided material for a lining, cut this with the aid of the jacket pattern.

*Making.*—Baste the seams of the jacket with close stitches. As the skirt has fulness at the waist line, the seams may be stitched before the first fitting. Baste these carefully before stitching and, after stitching, press them open. Leave the upper end of the left seam open for a placket, and finish this in a manner similar to the welt-seam placket, but omit the outside stitching and whip the facing in position.

After making the placket, gather the waist line of the skirt across the sides and back, leaving the front plain.

Make the straps as you would a double belt, but press them so that the seam is at the center.

*Fitting.*—Pin the skirt to the inside belting, adjusting the fulness to make it becoming and letting ½ inch or more of the skirt extend above the belting. Then turn the hem at the lower edge and pin the straps in position as you desire them, looping them under the skirt at the bottom. Also, determine what length the belt should be to fit easily over the skirt belting.

Observe the various points that should be noted in the fitting of the jacket. If the muslin model was carefully handled, you will probably find it necessary to make few, if any, changes.

*Finishing.*—Stitch the jacket seams, press them open, and bind the raw edges, provided you do not wish to line the coat, first notching them through the curved portions to make them lie perfectly flat. Make the collar double, first stitching and pressing open its center-back seams.

Make the pockets ready for application by facing the lower portions with the pieces provided for this purpose, turning under the allowance at the top and sides and covering the raw edges with silk facing strips if you are making the jacket of wool.

Try the coat on again, turn the lower edge of the jacket and of the sleeves, and pin the collar and pockets in position.

Secure the pockets by whipping the upper edge of the under facing portion to the lower edge of the jacket and securing the sides with very close slip-stitches or with machine stitching, if the material you are using will appear well with stitching.

If you have not provided a lining for the jacket, cover the raw edges turned at the bottom of the jacket and sleeves with narrow facing strips of silk, or merely turn hems, provided the suit material is silk. Also, join the collar as a binding.

If you have provided a lining, merely stitch the raw edges of the collar together to the coat and press these edges back on the coat. Then, after stitching and pressing open the seams of the lining, slip-stitch this to the coat so as to cover all the raw edges, which have first been catch-stitched flat.

To finish the skirt, turn the allowance made at the top over the belting, and then, with the belting turned out from the skirt, stitch the skirt to this and cover the raw edge with a facing.

Trim away the surplus strap material at the lower edge, leaving a generous ½ inch or more beyond the turned edge. Then trim away less than ¼ inch of the end of the strap next to the skirt hem, turn the other edge over this, and slip-stitch it flat to the under side of the hem. Also, slip-stitch the strap to the hem near the turned lower edge.

If the suit is of woolen material, bind the edge of the skirt hem instead of turning it under before securing it.

After making the belt, tack this to the waist line at several points, arranging the opening over the left side seam in line with the placket.

---

## Linings Evidence Quality

"Better no lining than one that compares unfavorably with the quality or distinctiveness of the coat fabric," seems to be the rule adopted for the coats of today, for many models are without linings and those which are lined evidence material that would grace even a dress design.

Crêpe de Chine of a firm, excellent quality seems to be the predominant lining fabric. Pussy-Willow taffeta is also highly favored, and when the coat is a part of a three-piece costume, the lining very often is of the same fabric as the upper dress portion.

As a general rule, however, the lining is of an unobtrusive color, unless it is used for a particular effect in a three-piece costume. Soft grays verging on the silver tones and a range of tans, from bisque to deeper tones, are the outstanding colors.

Figured and high-colored linings also have a place among lining fabrics, but are seldom found in the most distinctive suits.

Model 6

# Magic Pattern: *Mother Daughter Blouse*

This is an original Magic Pattern, a project you cut out using diagrams instead of pattern pieces. These were first created by Mary Brooks Picken for the Woman's Institute's student magazines, Inspiration and Fashion Service. My book **Vintage Notions: An Inspirational Guide to Needlework, Cooking, Sewing, Fashion & Fun** featured 12 original Magic Patterns. Recently I have created modern patterns that were inspired by these vintage gems featured in the book **The Magic Pattern Book**, which I licensed with Workman Publishing. We have chosen to keep the authenticity of this original pattern intact and therefore have not changed instructions based on modern fabrics and techniques. Note at the end of this pattern you will find helpful tips for drafting pattern pieces.

▶▶▶ FESTIVE COTTON BLOUSES for mother and daughter can be made in a few hours. For mother, buy twice the length from shoulder to waist plus ½ yd. for ruffle. For daughter, buy shoulder-to-waist length plus 10 in. for ruffle. Buy two 3-yd. packages of rick rack in contrasting colors, thread for each color, and elastic or tape for drawstrings.

*Mother's blouse:* Straighten fabric. Tear off two 8-in. crosswise strips for ruffle. On blouse piece measure in from selvage one-half the bust measurement plus 10 in.; tear off lengthwise strip. Fold blouse piece in half lengthwise. Mark center of fold A, as in diagram, and center of selvage B. On either side of A, measure along fold the length from shoulder to waist. For armhole, measure in from selvage one-third armhole measurement (B-C). Measure same amount to right and left of B for D and E. Mark curve as shown. Trim side seam, starting 1½ in. in at F and tapering to nothing at D. Mark darts as at G. Taper underarm and mark darts on back in same way. Cut from F to D around armhole and along underarm of back. Tear crosswise at A for back and front of blouse.

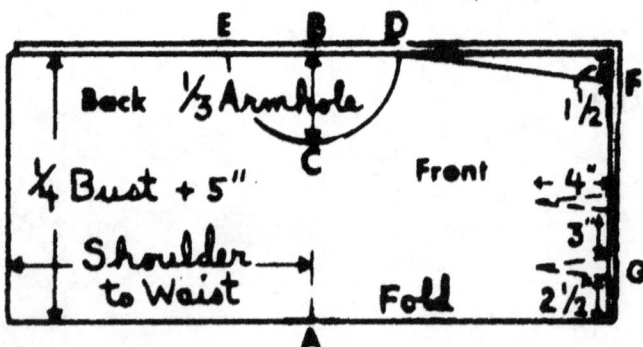

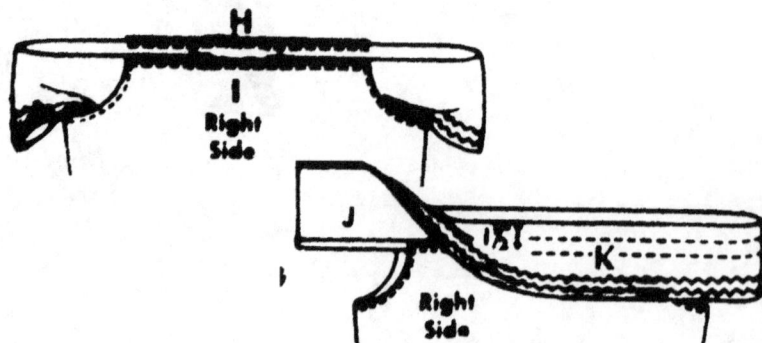

Seam selvages of ruffle strips together to make circle; finish one edge with ¼-in. hem. Apply rick rack over stitching and again 1 in. above. French-seam blouse sides. Finish armholes with narrow hems.

Place wrong side of blouse over right side of ruffle, matching center points, H and I. Stitch edges together across blouse top, as shown. Turn up ruffle and press seam, as at J. Bring ruffle to right side,

making a fold 1½ in. above seam.

Press fold. Stitch ruffle to blouse just below seam, as at K. Continue stitching across shoulder section and entirely around ruffle. Make second stitching ¾ in. above first to make casing. Work a buttonhole-type of opening at center-front of casing (on wrong side for elastic, right side for decorative drawstrings).

Stitch darts to shape waistline. Finish bottom edge with 1-in. hem casing and work an opening at center front of it.

Gather at neckline and waistline with drawstrings or elastic.

*Child's blouse:* Tear two 5-in. crosswise strips for ruffle. Same dimensions can be used for cutting, but allow only 5 in. to chest measurement. Make as above, except that waistline need not be darted.

# Your Measurement Chart & Notes on Making Magic Patterns

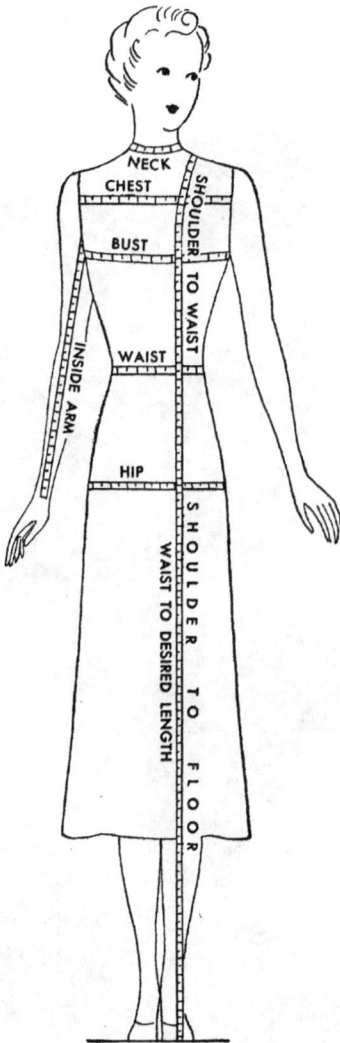

BUST (Fullest Part).............._____

WAIST ......................._____

HIP (Fullest Part) .............._____

WIDTH OF CHEST.............._____

FRONT WAIST LENGTH
Shoulder to Waist.............._____

FRONT SKIRT LENGTH
Waist to Desired Length........._____

FRONT FULL LENGTH
Shoulder to Floor .............._____

NECK (At Base) .............._____

SHOULDER
Neck to Armhole Line.........._____

ARMHOLE ..................._____

WIDTH OF BACK .............._____

BACK LENGTH
Neck to Waist ..............._____

BACK LENGTH
Neck to Floor................._____

OUTSIDE ARM
Shoulder to Wrist (Arm Bent)...._____

INSIDE ARM
Armhole to Wrist (Arm Straight).._____

UPPER ARM (Fullest Part)......._____

ELBOW (Arm Bent) ..........._____

WRIST ..................._____

HAND (Closed) .............._____

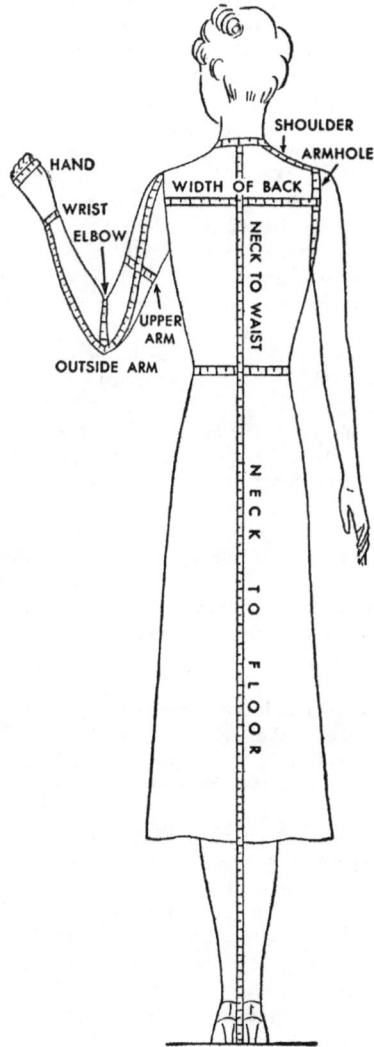

## Keep Accurate Measurements

Since the garments in this book are all cut from measurements, it is necessary to have accurate ones to follow. Keep a list of your own measurements always at hand for ready reference.

Measurements for fitted garments should be taken over the type of foundation garments you expect to wear with them. Remove dress, jacket, or coat, which would distort the measurements. Do not take measurements too tight. Make all easy enough for comfort. The chart shows how to place the tape correctly for each measurement.

## Making The Pattern

If you have the least doubt about your ability to chalk out the garment on your fabric, then rough it out first with crayon or heavy pencil on wrapping paper or newspaper. Cut out the paper pattern and use it to cut your garment. Cutting from a diagram, you can be sure that the proportions are correct for your size and that the garment will be a good fit.

# Little *Folks,* Big in *Appreciation*

*By* ALICE M. STONE
Editorial Department

"MY two most important reasons for wishing to learn to sew," writes a student whose picture shows her with a youngster on each knee. "*Our* most important reasons for wishing to learn to sew," echo thousands of students, the mothers of the little folks on this page and of other Institute kiddies.

"Children's clothes are so high, and you know you do love to have your child look as nice as your neighbor's," writes another student. Most mothers are human enough to recognize such a feeling—not that they wish to outdo their neighbors in any vainglorious way, but out of the love they bear their children there comes the desire to see that the little ones have every chance to appear at advantage among other children.

"I love the work and enjoy seeing my little girl wearing more becoming dresses than those I had when I went to school," writes still another student. "You can never know how much you have done for me and mine."

Because they have once been children themselves, mothers realize the acute discomfiture of childish hearts over being obliged to wear unbecoming clothes, and out of the greater wisdom of their years they realize, too, the subtle danger to a child's self-esteem through his habitual subjection to such discomfiture.

But they have seen the reverse side of the picture, too. They have watched the little mites gaze with rapt attention at some beautiful gown, sidling up, perhaps, and shyly caressing it with beauty-loving fingers. And they have experienced the joy of creating for such beauty-loving youngsters attractive garments that have made them proud and happy way down to the bottom of their stout little hearts.

OCCASIONALLY it has been some one besides the mother who has made the child happy in this way. I happen to recall a student out in Illinois, Mrs. Deborah De Baun.

"I had completed only my fifth lesson," she wrote, "when I decided to make a dress for a little tot I knew who did not have as many pretty dresses as other little two-to-three-year olds. One dress inspired me to two, the joy she got out of the pretty, dainty frocks more than paying me for my time and effort. She was as proud and pleased as any girl of sixteen.

"And then I learned that she did not have a warm coat and that coats down town cost $12.00 to $15.00. So I remembered an old tan camel's hair sport coat I had. I got it out, ripped it up, and washed it. When the coat was finished, it was so pretty and looked so near the "store kind" that I was delighted, and when I saw the wonder and appreciation in the mother's eyes, I thought surely no one could be happier than I."

"WHEN I announced I was going to make a winter coat for the boy of the house out of an out-of-style coat," writes Mrs. Violet E. Good, a California student, "I read despair on the faces of my family. They looked relieved, however, when I said that, unless it looked ready-made, he wouldn't have to wear it. Well, Sonny boy wears that coat and proudly announces to all that 'Mamma made it.' The only expense was $1.50 for lining and buttons and I couldn't get another under $12.00.

"For my little girl, I made a fully lined coat of all-wool polo cloth, costing me only $3.35. Both coats were copied from the most popular models offered. They have an additional advantage in that the hems and sleeves can be lengthened, which means the coats will be worn out instead of outgrown.

"My chief conceit, however, is over the things my scrap bag yields. From out-of-style dresses come good-looking knickers. Rompers are made from left-over pieces of material. Middies, step-ins, an adorable bloomer dress of pongee, and innumerable other things miraculously immerge from its depths, garments which, had I not learned to sew, we would have had to do without or pay a good price for."

THE picture would hardly be complete without some mention of the help that the mother's sewing is to the family. "Last winter," writes Mrs. George Dolloff, a Rhode Island student, "I made a chinchilla coat with mannish pockets and hat to match, costing about half the store prices, a poplin coat and bonnet smocked daintily with pink floss, a mackinaw coat for my oldest boy, from his father's overcoat, a suit of brown serge, the trousers properly lined and pocketed, and numerous other little garments.

"Our average expense for clothing for all the family falls within $20 a month and there are five of us.

"We began nearly seven years ago with a bonus of $100 each from a kindly State government and we have now a comfortable home, three children, an automobile, and $2,000 in the bank.

"Without being able to sew as I have, we could never have done so well, as we have loaned $400 to a sister for college and given another $400 as an alumnae gift.

"I claim that $1,000 anyway is what I have saved by my knowledge of dressmaking."

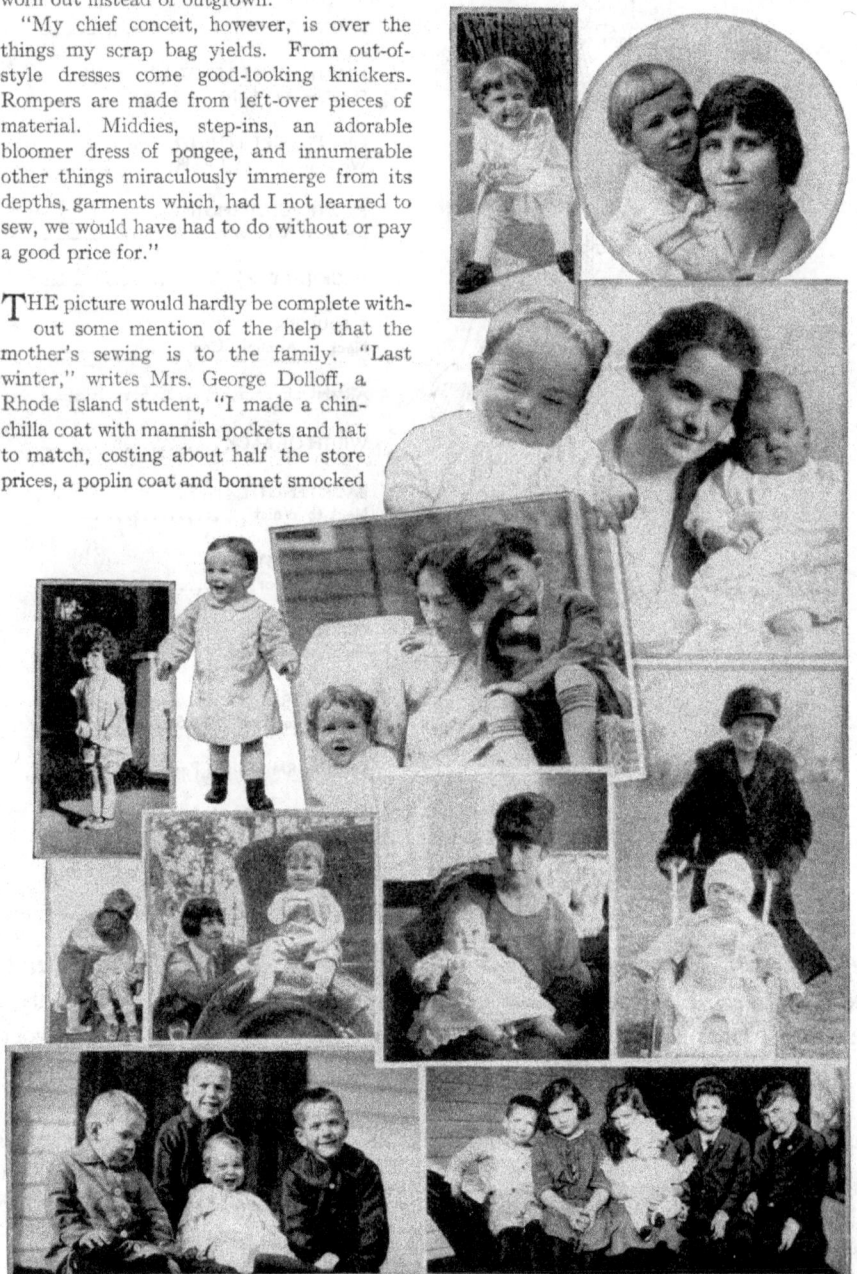

Originally published in *Inspiration* magazine, May 1926

# Simplicity in the Baby's Wardrobe

*By* MARGARET MURRIN
Department of Dressmaking

THE word simplicity may seem an over-worked term as applied to the first clothes for the "very youngest," particularly to the doting aunts and grandmothers who feel that nothing is too dainty or beautiful for the small treasure. But the young mother, despite the same feelings, realizes how much it means to have the entire wardrobe sensible as to cut and finish so that the little garments will be easy to put on and comfortable after they are on. However, even if simplicity *is* considered the most important quality in the baby's wardrobe, there is no need for monotony since the little garments may vary in cut and trimming and still conform to all the modern ideas of what the new baby should wear.

In the matter of dresses, one has a choice of three types; the kimono-sleeve, the raglan, and the set-in-sleeve. One of each type is illustrated to show variety both in cut and in trimming. Of course, when more than one dress is being made and time is a factor to be considered, quicker results may be had if one pattern is followed so that several garments may be cut at one time. If this plan seems best, consider the merits of each and then decide on the style that suits your needs and the requirements of its young wearer, following it for all the little dresses with variation in the trimming only.

No matter what style of dress is to be made, the same points concerning the texture and quality of the material apply because certain rules pertaining to both common sense and comfort must be observed. The first requisite is softness of weave, with reasonable sheerness and sufficient firmness. Ease of laundering, too, is an important point.

THE firm, sheer qualities of batiste, nainsook, and the finer long-cloths, having all of these qualities, prove to be satisfactory materials for the purpose. Lawn in the softest weaves is good, too, while for certain types of dresses, fine handkerchief linen is sometimes used. But the fact that this fabric crushes so readily makes it objectionable.

The amount of material needed depends somewhat on the finished length of the little dress. Most infants' dress patterns are cut 24 inches long plus hem allowance, although dresses as short as 22 inches or as long as 27 inches are considered satisfactory, it being understood that the baby born during the warm months does not require the length in his dresses that the winter baby does. The average amount of material, however, will vary from 1⅝ to 1¾ yards, the latter amount being sufficient to cut a 27-inch dress. For either the kimono-sleeve or the raglan-sleeve type, ⅛ yard more is required than for the dress with set-in sleeves.

Trimming on the little frocks should be simple. Small sprays of fine embroidery, hemstitching, feather-stitching, fine tucks, and very narrow lace edgings are all appropriate, for besides the fact that elaborate trimming is not in good taste, there is also the feature that the dresses are outgrown so rapidly that a great deal of hand-work on them is really a waste of time. Let your plan be to have the materials as fine as you can afford, the hand-work dainty, and the trimming restrained, so that the finished effect will be one of simplicity and distinction.

OF the three types of dresses, that cut with the kimono sleeve, illustrated at the left, has the advantage of ease of ironing as well as ease of putting on and taking off. It is also the simplest type of dress to make.

In making it, finish the under-arm seam with a flat fell either by hand or by machine. After applying the continuous placket as the back opening, finish the gathered neck line and the lower edge of the sleeve with straight and very narrow bands, trimming these in turn with a narrow lace edge applied by hand with only slight fulness. Turn a hem, measuring from 2½ to 3 inches deep, and put it in by hand.

You may let your own fancy dictate to you the kind and amount of embroidery you apply. In the little dress illustrated, a combination of hand hemstitching and French embroidery is used. A similar motif may be applied just above the hem if a somewhat more elaborate effect is desired.

*Pictorial Review* pattern No. 1369 duplicates this style and contains also patterns for a complete layette.

THE raglan-sleeve model, illustrated at the right, has many of the advantages of the kimono-sleeve garment with additional smartness because a little of the excess material at the shoulder and under arm is taken out by the seams that form the raglan effect.

In making this little dress, use tiny French seams to join the sleeves to the dress as well as for the under-arm and sleeve seams. Finish the back opening with a flat-stitched placket, and, after gathering the neck edge, apply the collar with a narrow bias facing. This type of collar is usually worn by boy babies; so if the little dress is intended for a baby girl, you may prefer to use a narrow band with fine lace edging. Attach cuffs or a band as a finish for the lower edge of the sleeves. You will notice that a scalloped edge is used on both the collar and the cuffs, this being a very dainty finish for such garments.

After turning up the 3-inch hem and sewing it carefully in place by hand, apply the embroidery, although if you find it easier, this hand-work may all be completed after the dress is cut but before it is sewed together.

McCall pattern No. 2367 may be used as a cutting guide in developing this little garment as well as a Gertrude petticoat.

THE set-in sleeve dress, illustrated in the center, is a little more difficult to make than either of the other two types discussed, but is preferred by many mothers because of its trim good looks. Then, too, a dress of this cut is very satisfactory for wear under sweaters or coats, since it will lie flat and smooth without any bunchiness.

After tucking the front and applying the feather-stitching that trims it, join the shoulder and under arms of both dress and sleeve with French seams, or for a very smooth effect, use flat-fell seams. Insert the sleeves, using French-seams, and finish their lower edges with hems held in place by feather-stitching.

Before applying the neck band, finish the back opening with a short-lapped placket, which may be fastened with buttonholes and small buttons or left open with a fastening at the neck line only. The neck band, in this case, consists of a straight band finished with lace edging, but if preferred, a small collar, cut double, stitched, and turned, may be used. Finish such a collar with a row of feather-stitching placed ¼ inch inside the edge. Turning and stitching the hem will complete the dress.

*Pictorial Review* pattern No. 3472 provides a satisfactory cutting guide for this style and contains as well a raglan-sleeve dress pattern that may be used for the little dress cut over these lines, also patterns for most of the other little garments necessary for a complete layette.

# Song of the Needle

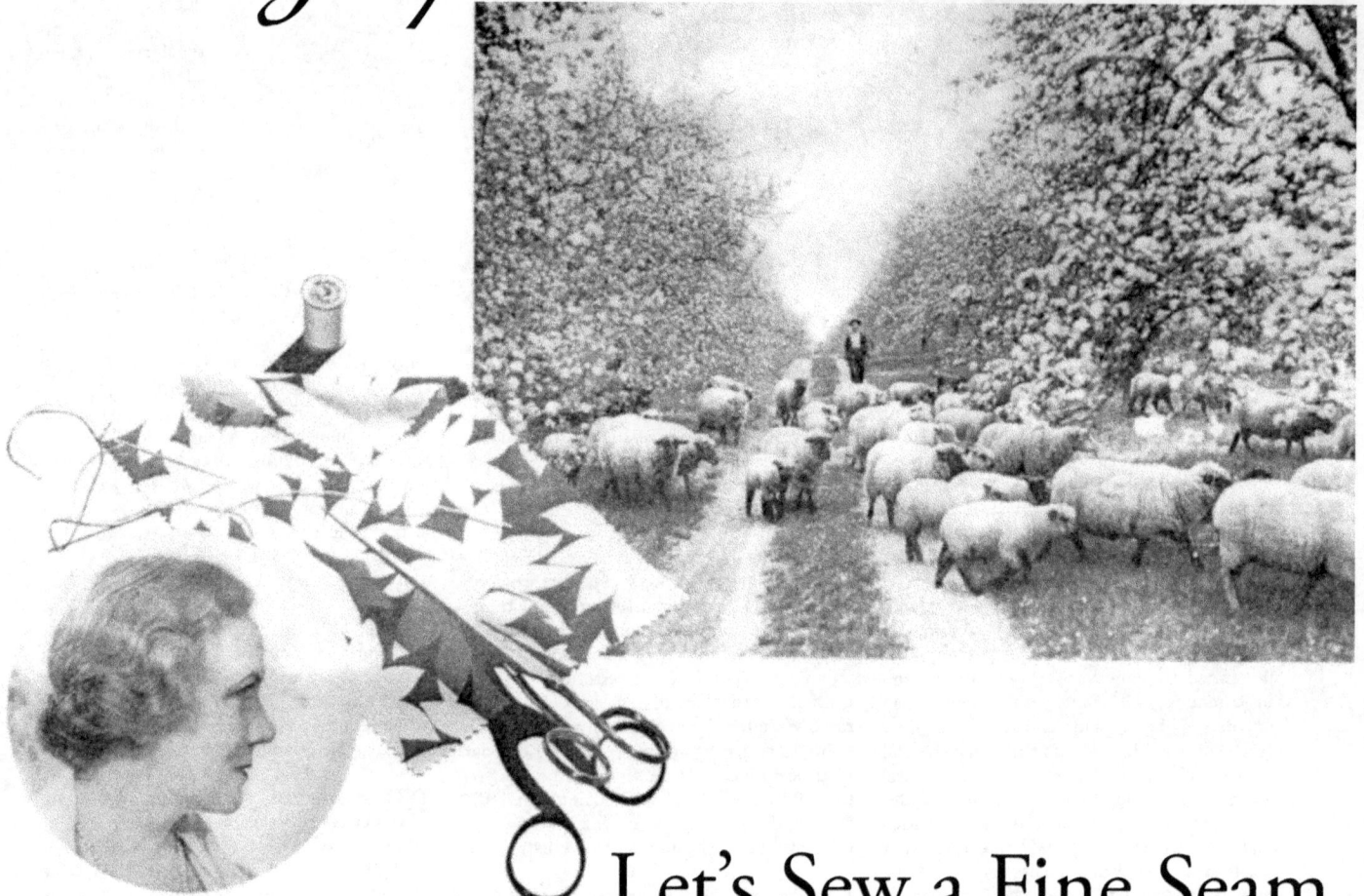

## Let's Sew a Fine Seam

### By MARY BROOKS PICKEN

All my life, as a student, as a teacher, as a writer, I have worked with women. Especially have I sought to find the greatest common denominator of their interests. And I think I have found it in the almost universal desire for self-expression.

For many years I directed the work of the largest educational institution in the world engaged in teaching women in the home. During a period of nine years, actually five percent of all the women in the United States wrote to us seeking help. For a time I was in almost constant contact with nearly a quarter of a million women and girls. My daily mail was a revelation of their hopes and ambitions. They wanted to express their desire to be attractive, and they found the way in the needle and in the use of beautiful fabrics.

Sometimes we hear discussions as to whether women dress themselves for men or for other women. I believe that neither of these reasons is important. I believe that women dress themselves for the soul-satisfaction they find in expressing beauty.

Some women can paint beautiful pictures, some can write beautiful poetry or prose, some have a talent for music. Only a few are creative in these fields. But the needle provides a common language which is given to us all to use and enjoy.

Article written by Mary Brooks Picken, May 1935

I remember my own pride in the very first dress I ever made. I was fortunate in having a grandmother who was expert in spinning, weaving, sewing, and cooking. She had an innate love of materials that came from her own creative instinct, and a thorough knowledge of how fabrics were made. I learned as a very little girl to share with her an appreciation of the infinite care that went into the weaving of fabrics.

Grandmother told me something I have never forgotten—that "environment is the warp of life; education the woof; and experience the pattern."

One thing that Grandmother always insisted on when she was weaving fabric was to have the very best quality of wool or flax or cotton that she could obtain. The integrity of the fiber itself is what makes a fabric permanently beautiful, whether it be an exquisite piece of taffeta, a lustrous satin, or a fine wool or cotton. When I feel a piece of quality fabric on the piece goods counter, I have profound respect for everyone who had a part in its making because someone, 'way back at the beginning, insisted on fine fibers which both inspired and made possible the fine weaving and finishing and dyeing, and, ultimately, a splendid garment for someone to enjoy. When I see a shabby material, limp and lifeless and without beauty, I know that its shabbiness goes all the way back to the fiber from which it was woven.

And surely the pattern of life is much like that of a fabric. When I think of the thousands of women who have met and risen above the problems of the depression years, when I see women every day accomplishing true greatness in the shaping of their own lives, often in spite of the greatest handicaps, I know that within them there is an integrity of material that makes the richness of such patterns possible.

Grandmother wove many, many things for her own household. She was equally expert in the arts of the needle. I have taught many women to make a knot in thread as she did, and have urged that they buy needles and thread of the correct sizes for beautiful work. These were things I learned when I first learned to sew.

When I was eager to make a dress for myself, Grandmother wanted me to have a sense of the value of the material. So I bought three yards of 27-inch calico at one dozen eggs per yard. I gathered up the eggs day after day until I had enough. Grandmother could easily have given the material to me, but she knew that by earning it I would treasure it the more.

Later on, we ripped and pressed a navy blue wool skirt of Grandmother's to make a school dress for me. First she showed me a picture of sheep in her Bible and told me about wool. She taught me how to card wool and how to spin the yarn for weaving, how to dye fabrics and assemble colors, and how actually to weave.

I often regret that all women cannot know more of how the fabrics which they wear and with which they work are made. Their enthusiasm would be stimulated, and they would take even greater pride in the dresses they fashion from the yards of tempting materials they now find so conveniently waiting for them on the store counter. Perhaps it is too much to hope that children might again be taught very early—no matter what their station in life— those homely arts that give them a sense of values, not only of fabrics, but of all those accomplishments that make for human happiness—to make a bed so that it is comfortable to sleep in, to darn a stocking so that it comfortable to wear, to make a pie so that its aroma will thrill the whole household.

I can remember standing on a footstool watching my grandmother make a pie. She told me a pie could be gay or sad, and that could impart its character to the person who ate it. She showed me the flour and lard she was using, how white and fine they were, and told me of the delicacies these things would make. Then she turned to a picture on the wall and told me how the artist had mixed his colors to create a beautiful picture. She explained that he had to proportion all the colors perfectly to have it right.

Then she explained that it was just as necessary to use the right ingredients in the right quantities in the pie. Her pie crust formula I have used thousands of times successfully—ice-cold water, firm white lard, a generous pinch of salt, and,

Article written by Mary Brooks Picken, May 1935

in mixing, twice as much flour as lard and half as much water. Mix, lightly dust the immaculately clean bread board with flour, roll out the dough, and a gay pie crust results.

Yes, to make such a pie is another medium of self-expression. But it has been my observation that sewing has the most universal appeal for women, and it has been of great satisfaction to me during the last few years of depression that they have turned to it again. Girls who never had thought of making their own clothes now warm almost instinctively to sewing, and once the fascination of its creative qualities captures them they plunge into it with all the enthusiasm of youth. Women who have not sewed for years are taking it up again, just as many are turning again to knitting and crocheting, as variations of the creative urge. And I know of women past sixty who are just learning to sew. One dear white haired old lady called up a friend to say excitedly: "Janie, I'm happy—I've just learned what those notches and perforations in a pattern are for. I have just cut out a dress all by myself and know just how it goes together."

My faith in women finds its justification, too, in the spirit of those who carry the responsibility of leadership in creative work. I refer especially to the organization known as the Fashion Group. In 1930 a relatively new profession had achieved importance in the world of women's work. It included those who, through education, training, and experience, held positions of influence in fashion work in the fields of industrial designing, merchandising, advertising, selling, editing, and teaching.

A small group of people in these fields recognized that such fashion workers had a great opportunity to set standards for design and workmanship that would benefit all, especially women.

It established a new professional group which encourages those who are ambitious to develop their talents in the fields which the Fashion Group embraces. This group now includes in its membership nearly seven hundred women in America and Europe. They have shown an almost unprecedented quality of cooperation. Even though engaged competitively in business, they are working closely together and giving generously of time and effort in advancing this important new development among women. They are making a direct contribution of great importance to the future of all women engaged in any way in fashion work, and, indirectly, stimulating a keener enjoyment of creative expression by all women in the home.

Article written by Mary Brooks Picken, May 1935

*Vintage Notions Monthly* continues to share the work of Mary Brooks Picken and the Woman's Institute which inspired my book *Vintage Notions*. Although the Institute was founded 100 years ago, the treasure trove of lessons and stories are still relevant today and offer a blueprint for living a contented life.

If you enjoyed this issue of *Vintage Notions Monthly*, visit AmyBarickman.com for more of my curated collection of vintage content including patterns and books for needle and thread, inspiring fabric and textiles & free vintage art every Friday. Be sure to tune in to *Vintage Notions* episodes for a guided tour through my collection of sewing and fashion history, as well as modern projects inspired by my extensive library.

**www.amybarickman.com**

Find free images, inspiration and books for the sewing and needle arts!

**www.indygojunction.com**

Featuring digital & print patterns, books, tutorials, giveaways, project ideas, & more!

Subscribe to each of our eNewsletters to learn about new products, receive special offers, discounts, videos, and get a FREE eBook!

Vintage Notions Monthly , Volume 1, Issue 5  (VN0105)

For wholesale ordering information contact Amy Barickman, LLC at 913.341.5559 or amyb@amybarickman.com, P.O. Box 30238, Kansas City, MO 64112